MAIL
SURVEYS

**Applied Social Research Methods Series
Volume 40**

APPLIED SOCIAL RESEARCH METHODS SERIES

MAIL SURVEYS

Improving the Quality

Thomas W. Mangione

Applied Social Research Methods Series
Volume 40

SAGE Publications
International Educational and Professional Publisher
Thousand Oaks   London   New Delhi

For information address:

 SAGE Publications, Inc.
2455 Teller Road
Thousand Oaks, California 91320
E-mail: order@sagepub.com

SAGE Publications Ltd.
6 Bonhill Street
London EC2A 4PU
United Kingdom

SAGE Publications India Pvt. Ltd.
M-32 Market
Greater Kailash I
New Delhi 110 048 India

Printed in the United States of America

Library of Congress Cataloging-in-Publication Data

Mangione, Thomas W.
  Mail surveys: Improving the quality / Thomas W. Mangione.
    p. cm. — (Applied social research methods series; v. 40)
  Includes bibliographical references (pp. 117-124) and index.
  ISBN 0-8039-4662-7 (alk. paper). — ISBN 0-8039-4663-5 (pbk.:
alk. paper)
    1. Mail surveys.   I. Title. II. Series.
  H62.M2359   1995
  001.4′33—dc20   95-9378

This book is printed on acid-free paper.

95 96 97 98 99 10 9 8 7 6 5 4 3 2 1

Sage Project Editor: Susan McElroy

Contents

List of Figures

Preface

Writing a text about mail survey techniques caps an interesting evolution in my regard for alternate survey data collection techniques. When I was first trained in survey methodology in the late 1960s and early 1970s at the University of Michigan's Survey Research Center, there was really only one method to consider to produce high quality data—the in-person interview. However, as phone ownership increased and we developed random digit dialing techniques, telephone surveys became the strategy of choice. Phone studies reflected an optimum trade-off between cost and quality. Mail surveys have always been considered the least preferred data collection process primarily because of concerns about response rate problems.

There is a growing body of research, however, that tells us that there are ways and circumstances to conduct mail surveys that do produce high quality results. I have become a firm believer in the potential of mail surveys to provide quality information. My goal in writing this book is to provide a concise summary of the key elements necessary to conduct a mail survey study. You will discover as you read this book that ensuring high quality from a mail survey study involves more than knowing about inducing good response rates; it also involves reducing other sources of error such as sampling bias and question response errors. This book points to the need to consider all these factors at once to succeed.

I wish to acknowledge two of my mentors who played a critical role in the socialization and honing of my survey skills. Robert (Rob) P. Quinn was my mentor at the University of Michigan. I had the opportunity to learn from Rob how to make a survey not only understandable but also a work of art. Rob excelled in one key element of mentorship: He gave you room to try it yourself and then provided criticism in a constructive environment when refining your work.

My first 18 years of postdoctorate survey efforts were spent working side by side with Floyd J. (Jack) Fowler, Jr. Jack was also a Michigan graduate, so we shared a similar research socialization history. During our years together at the Center for Survey Research at the University of Massachusetts–Boston, I found Jack to be unfailing in his championing of high quality data collection efforts.

Both Rob and Jack taught me an important lesson about data quality, though. Not only is it an appropriate goal, but you can also help others achieve high quality in their own work if you respect their research goals and share with them your enthusiasm for the techniques that produce quality. Rob and Jack were always enthusiastic about data quality. In this regard this book owes much to them.

There are many others who made direct and indirect contributions to the production of this book whom I would like to acknowledge. Over the past 15 years I have taught classes in survey research methods at both Boston University and Harvard University's Schools of Public Health. There is no better way to keep one's focus on data collection quality than to routinely face a class of graduate students and try to articulate to them how to do surveys well. Much of what I say in this text has been developed in my class lectures. I owe a debt to my students for helping me to crystallize my message. In particular I want to acknowledge the efforts of my 1991 Harvard class who aided in the search for, and summarizing of, a variety of research articles about improving mail surveys.

I also want to acknowledge the support provided by my current employer, JSI (John Snow Inc.) Research and Training Institute and in particular Joel Lamstein as president and Patricia Fairchild as vice-president and director of my division. They encouraged me to produce this book and were understanding when its production took my time and company resources. I was aided by several staff at JSI whose contributions were appreciated. Jane Ryan helped design the figures in this text and provided the initial efforts to pull together the bibliography. Denise Yob also helped with the design of the figures. Deborah LeBel helped with proofreading. Teresa Frydryk has spent hours helping me complete the bibliography and checking the accuracy of the citations.

I also want to thank my family (Kathy, Christy, and Lisa) for their patience and support over the years when I have had to work on weekends to help improve the quality of a study's data collection effort.

Finally, I want to say that this book may read differently from many textbooks you have seen before. It will sound like you are sitting in my class, hearing a lecture from me. It will sound very pragmatic. You should feel that you have learned the skills necessary to produce a high quality mail survey when you have completed reading it. This was done purposively because it is my style. I want to thank the series' editors, Len Bickman and Debra Rog, for their support in this regard.

1

Introduction

WHEN IS A MAIL SURVEY
THE RIGHT CHOICE?

This book is a short treatise on how to do mail surveys. Before you use it, though, you first need to decide whether a mailed survey is the appropriate data collection strategy for your research problem. Although you will be better able to answer this question at the end of the book, at this point I would like to give you a flavor of the appropriate situations to use mail surveys.

It is a good idea to consider using mail surveys when:

1. your research sample is widely distributed geographically,
2. your research budget is modest,
3. you want to give your research subjects time to think about their answers,
4. your questions are written in a closed-ended style,
5. your research sample has a moderate to high investment in the topic,
6. your list of research objectives is modest in length,
7. you want to give your research subjects privacy in answering,
8. your questions work better in a visual rather than oral mode, and
9. you have limited person-power to help you conduct your study.

You may think of other good reasons as you read this book.

THE SCOPE OF THIS BOOK

This book is intended to accomplish one basic goal: to provide the reader with a straightforward, pragmatic guide to conducting mail surveys. In meeting this goal, I discuss this method in contrast to other data collection methods such as in-person interviews or telephone surveys. There are many design circumstances that would suggest that these other data collection techniques should be the strategy of choice.

1

Other books in this series do an admirable job of helping the researcher conduct surveys using these other methods (see Fowler, 1993; Lavrakas, 1993).

My focus does not encompass directly all self-administered data collection techniques. My central goal is explaining mail survey techniques. In limiting myself this way, I can provide more information about the techniques necessary to accomplish a high quality mail survey data collection. In detailing these procedures, though, it turns out that much of the information presented also applies to other research circumstances including the broader range of self-administered formats such as group administrations.

One thing is paramount in the organization of the materials in this book. The emphasis is on describing how to do high quality research. Sometimes quality is assumed to mean expensive, and to a certain degree that is true. To the extent that being careful or complete requires resources and therefore money, then designing for quality means a more expensive design. However, not all quality goals require additional resources to achieve them. Sometimes it just takes planning and careful consideration. Sometimes it just means not rushing. Sometimes it means getting another opinion. Sometimes it just means being clear in your own mind about what you are trying to accomplish.

Interestingly enough, sometimes the quick and dirty surveys are the most expensive of all when value is considered. If the quick and dirty method produces information that is invalid, useless, and misleading, then whatever you paid to get it accomplished was too much. Instead, designing a survey that produces high quality information will give you good value for your dollar, and it becomes a truly efficient method of data collection.

WHY IS A BOOK ONLY
ABOUT MAIL SURVEYS NECESSARY?

The answer to this question is simple: The world is filled with examples of poor quality mail surveys. Mail surveys are seductive in their apparent simplicity—type up some questions, reproduce them, address them to respondents, wait for returns to come in, and then analyze the answers. Any survey process, however, contains many important steps that need to be considered carefully and carried out in a particular sequence. Not knowing what these steps are leaves you vulnerable to producing a poor quality product.

There are many reasons that people get pushed into doing poor quality work. Certainly time pressure is one reason, but perhaps the biggest cause is ignorance—not knowing the negative consequences of a decision. To give you an idea of what these problems might be, we describe two examples of problematic mail surveys; they are presented not with the intent of ridiculing or pointing fingers, but instead to heighten your awareness of the need for understanding and preparation.

Example 1: The *Literary Digest*'s Miscalling of the 1936 Election

This example is a legend in the field of survey research. It encompasses one of the most dramatic and public research failures of modern times, and the basic story is part of American political folklore. What is doubly important for our purpose is that most explanations of the problem with this study themselves misidentify the culprit (Bryson, 1976).

The *Literary Digest* had made a reputation for itself by publishing, before a presidential election, the results of a poll it conducted predicting the winner of the upcoming election. In 1936 the *Literary Digest* definitively predicted that Landon would defeat Roosevelt. Of course, as we all know, Roosevelt was instead elected to a second term by a wide margin. How could the poll have been so wrong? Most current explanations for the poll's failure focus on the sampling strategy and describe the study as one that was limited to people who owned telephones. The common explanation is that by surveying people who owned a telephone, and by collecting the data by telephone, the poll reached only a select segment of the voting population, a largely Republican strata.

The common explanations about this study are wrong in several respects. First the sample was not limited to people who owned telephones. The sample came from several sources—telephone books, automobile registrations, and voter registration lists. The sample was a reasonable attempt to encompass the voting population. Second, the data collection method was not the telephone but instead a mail survey! So the *Literary Digest* conducted a mail survey and it mispredicted the election. Why? The answer is straightforward: The data were based on a biased segment of the population, *not* because the sample selected was biased, but rather because the sample *returning* the surveys was biased. The *Digest* poll had a response rate of only 23%. The problem was that Landon supporters were more likely to respond than Roosevelt supporters and therefore the data contained a fatal and, unfortunately, very publicly displayed flaw.

Example 2: The Sheri Hite Sexual Behavior Study

In the mid-1970s Dr. Sheri Hite conducted a study of female sexual behavior that became enormously popular (Hite, 1976). Dr. Hite's method was to distribute mail-back surveys to as wide an audience as possible by printing them in a variety of magazines and distributing them through groups. About 100,000 questionnaires were distributed and approximately 3,000 were returned, for a response rate of 3%. Again, low response rates might raise doubts about the study's findings. Because the vast majority of potential respondents did not return the survey, it is likely that the small minority who did return the surveys were somehow different from the general population. Of course we can't know this for sure, but it does cast doubts about the findings.

The Hite study had more methodological problems. Dr. Hite created a questionnaire that used exclusively open-ended question formats. This made the task of responding to the questions more difficult and the task of extracting information systematically from the responses more challenging. Clearly, this was one factor that discouraged some people from responding. It is one thing to ask people to check off 70 boxes or so; it is quite another thing to ask them to write mini-essays on 70 different topics.

Also, the questions themselves created problems. Some of the questions used wording that used the common vernacular for various body parts, and this might have put off some potential respondents. Sometimes respondents could choose which part of a question they wanted to respond to and hence it was hard to compare answers across individuals.

This study is an example of how multiple methodological problems can easily come together in one study and cast serious doubts on the value of the study as a valid representation of the population.

PROBLEMS TO AVOID

From these two examples the reader can get a feel for the types of problems and issues that might arise when conducting a mail survey. The following chapters should help you to avoid major pitfalls. In broad brush strokes, the areas where problems are most likely to arise fall into four categories:

1. One common problem area is *sample selection bias*. A major fault is using a list to draw a sample that is incomplete in a significant

way. Sometimes the list is out of date. People may have left and new people may have arrived, but the list you use does not represent the recent changes. Obviously, sampling from outdated lists will produce outdated samples.

Sometimes the problem with the list is more subtle. You might use the wrong list. For instance, if you want to find out why people may or may not use a neighborhood health center, you might be tempted to draw a sample from patient files—some who have visited recently and some who have not. The real question being asked is "Why do people who live in the neighborhood either use the health center or not?" Therefore, the sample that is most appropriate is a sample of neighborhood residents, not a sample of health center clients. Making sure that your list corresponds to the population you want to study is a critical point on the road to quality data.

2. A second problem area involving sampling relates to the *biased nature of the responding sample*. It doesn't matter how accurately and randomly you draw a sample if it turns out that returns come mainly from people biased in a particular way. Unfortunately, it is sometimes hard to know whether the responding sample is biased. The standard safeguard is to try to achieve a high response rate, somewhere near 75% or higher if possible. With this type of response rate, the nonresponders would have to be very different from the responders in order to affect your overall estimates for the population.

3. Another general problem area is the *failure of respondents to answer individual questions*—they leave them blank, they accidentally skip over them, they don't follow instructions and so fill out the answers incorrectly, or they write marginal comments that can't be equated with your printed answer categories. If this happens often enough, your remaining data may again be biased.

4. The final broad area of problems comes from *respondents misunderstanding the wording of the questions as presented*. The central tenet of quantitative survey research is that everybody understands the question in the same way and can provide an answer to the question. This is a simply stated goal, yet it is sometimes frustratingly difficult to achieve. Two general themes will help you write good questions—make it clear and don't go beyond what is reasonable to expect people to remember. We have lots of new tools that are helping us reach our goals for valid questions, but still it takes effort to get there (Fowler, 1995).

By describing these four broad areas in which problems may arise, I also introduce an important goal that you should keep in mind as you use this book. It is important to design quality into all stages and parts of your mail survey project. If you cut corners in one area in order to do an excellent job in another, the final product may still have significant quality problems. Quality is not an average of the efforts that you put in but rather is achieved only by showing concern for all phases of the project. This notion of optimizing your efforts across all areas is referred to as "total survey design" (Biemer, Groves, Lyberg, Mathiowetz, & Sudman, 1991). I emphasize in each chapter how to produce quality in specific areas, but in the last chapter, I remind you that you have to put it all together to end up with a quality product.

ADVANTAGES OF MAIL SURVEYS

Although there are many problems to overcome and many pitfalls lurking for the uneducated researcher, a mail survey is a very appropriate way of gathering data and can produce high quality information. As a reminder, the advantages of mail surveys over other methods of data collection include:

1. they are relatively inexpensive,
2. they allow for large numbers of respondents to be surveyed in a relatively short period,
3. they allow respondents to take their time in answering and look up information if need be,
4. they give privacy in responding,
5. they allow for visual input rather than merely auditory input,
6. they allow the respondent to answer questions at times that are convenient,
7. they allow the respondent to see the context of a series of questions, and
8. they insulate the respondent from the expectations of the interviewer.

AN OVERVIEW OF
THE MAIL SURVEY PROCESS

As the final segment of our introduction, I want to give you a sense of what the steps might be in conducting a mail survey. The subsequent chapters will then provide you with information on how to accomplish these various steps. The first step is to develop the research goals for a study. What do you want to accomplish? What issues do you want to address in your study? As one figures out the "what" and the "who" of the survey process, the plausible alternative methods for collecting data become more apparent. Often at this stage, one will select a mail survey process as the data collection mechanism.

From here, two processes go on in parallel. One is the development of the questionnaire and the other is the selection of the sample. Selecting the sample involves defining your population, obtaining a list of the population, randomly selecting a sample, and preparing mailing labels for your sample. Developing your questionnaire involves becoming much more specific about the goals of your study, particularly in terms of the specific pieces of information you will need to answer your research questions. Using a detailed outline to guide you in the construction of your survey will prove invaluable. Working on the wording of individual questions involves an iterative process—draft the question, try it out, evaluate its performance, and revise if need be (sometimes many times).

Your questionnaire turns out to be more than merely a list of questions. The flow of the questionnaire, the logical sequence of questions, the format of your answer categories, and the style of the whole questionnaire become issues that deserve your attention at this stage.

Getting your data collected involves careful clerical procedures—making sure the right materials go in the right envelope so they can get to the right person is important. You'll have decided by this time the sequence of mailings and reminders, and what kind of incentives you will provide to respondents. The respondent letters that accompany the survey will have been carefully crafted.

As the surveys come back, it is important to keep careful track of who has responded and who has not. Reminders must be sent to those who haven't completed their survey. The information in the questionnaires is then translated into numbers for analysis by computer through a process of code development, coding, "keypunching," and software specifications for your data. Finally, your data are prepared for analysis by cleaning up any inconsistencies and correcting any errors made by coders or keypunchers. Analysis and report writing are the final steps in the research process.

2

The Basics of Question Design

In this chapter we will cover the basics of question design. How do you go from several blank pages to a series of questions that people can respond to and to which others will want to know the answers? First we'll start with structure—the form of the question. In particular, we'll describe the alternate types of questions you might use. Second, we'll talk about the content of the questions and how you can write a question that efficiently meets your question objectives.

TYPES OF QUESTIONS

In the world of survey design there are two broad classes of questions—open-ended questions and closed-ended questions. Open questions are ones that are asked with no specific categories of response given; instead the respondents answer in their own words. Closed-ended questions not only give the question but also present response alternatives; the respondent is encouraged to pick the answer that best represents his or her situation.

Open-Ended Questions

Let's start with open-ended questions. There are really two sub-categories of open-ended questions—short, specific answer types and longer, narrative types. An example of a short, specific answer type is the question "What is your current age?" followed by a line on which to record one's age. These types of questions are used in circumstances where the list of all possible answers is so large that it is impractical to put a check box response for each one. They work reasonably well as long as the answer needed is relatively short. Other examples are "What college did you attend?" or "What state were you born in?" The only problems with collecting information this way are that legibility of handwriting sometimes interferes with using the information and misunderstandings sometimes result in useless answers. For instance, "How do you get to work?" may result in an answer such as "I take the route down by the river" when instead you wanted to know the mode of transportation.

The other type of open-ended question is the narrative answer type. This is a question that requires a response that is more lengthy—a sentence or two or even a paragraph. These types of open-ended questions do not work very well in self-administered questionnaires. The big problem is that many respondents leave them blank; maybe only between 25% and 50% of the respondents will answer these questions. Among those that do answer, you may face additional problems with handwriting and answers that have inadequate detail. A response to the question "Why did you leave your old neighborhood?" may be "the people were getting to me." In order to actually use this answer you would need to know which people were being referred to and also in what way they were "getting to" the respondent.

These problems are so severe with narrative open questions that my recommendation is to avoid them. The only times I could see a use for them would be in circumstances where you wanted to be polite or at the end of a survey, as an "anything else" type of question. For instance, you might ask: "Have you received any awards in the past year?" with a yes/no check box. If the person answers yes, you should be polite and ask a follow-up question as to what the award was.

Closed-Ended Questions

There are several different types of closed-ended questions; I'll describe the most commonly used types.

Yes-No Questions

The simplest type of closed question is a "YES-NO" question. We get asked such questions dozens of times a day. The format is quite straightforward. Ask the question and provide two boxes to choose from—a "yes" and a "no." There is a variation on the "YES-NO" question that is a "CHECKLIST" with a box to check *only if* your answer is "yes." These are common when you have a long list of things within a group that you want people to easily go through. You've probably seen a list like this if you've ever filled out a medical history requesting "Check below all the diseases and conditions you had as a child."

The only concern I have about CHECKLISTS is that you can't distinguish a "no" response from an "accidentally skipped" response or a "don't know" response. To be perfectly clear, I recommend even in a checklist format that you present *both* the "yes" and the "no" box. I also think that forcing respondents to answer either a "yes" or a "no" will make them consider their answer just a tiny bit longer, which is probably good.

Close cousins to the YES-NO question are the TRUE-FALSE and the AGREE-DISAGREE questions.

Multiple Choice Questions

Another familiar type of question is the MULTIPLE CHOICE format. Any student has experience with these. They are the staples of many midterm exams. The key to constructing a good multiple choice question is that the categories you offer should be mutually exclusive and should cover the range of alternatives that people would experience. The final section of this chapter will talk about ways that you can make sure that you meet these criteria. Probably with these types of questions it is a good idea to put a little reminder that says "CHECK ONE ANSWER." If it turns out that multiple answers are possible, you could allow multiple checks (again with an instruction that says so), or you could turn each alternative into a "YES-NO" question. Every once in a while you might include as one of the choices a category of "other." With luck this will not be a frequently used category because it would make one curious as to what ideas were being included in that response. Sometimes researchers put a line beside the "other" saying "explain" or "specify." Now this follow-up question uses an OPEN-ENDED question format and becomes subject to the concerns raised above.

Semantic Differential

Another type of question is the SEMANTIC DIFFERENTIAL format. In this format respondents are usually asked to describe an object (e.g., their doctor, their spouse, their boss, their own moods, etc.). The question involves a series of opposite adjectives and an instruction to select a number between 1 and 7 (for example) that best describes how you feel.

sharp	1 2 3 4 5 6 7	dull
warm	1 2 3 4 5 6 7	cold
smart	1 2 3 4 5 6 7	dumb

Sometimes researchers get more complex with this type of question and ask people to answer it twice: once for your "current" boss and once for your "ideal" boss. Then they compare the two ratings and calculate a difference (or differential). The bigger the difference the less "satisfied" one presumably is with the current situation. You can use variations of this two rating procedure if you want to assess how things are "now" and how they were "5 years ago."

Ranking

Another format is the RANKING question. In this type of question you want the respondent to rank preferences among a group of alternatives, for example: "Among the reasons for choosing this college that are listed below, rank your reasons from most important to least important." You'll find that ranking questions work best if you don't give people too many things to rank order. A list of between 3 and 7 items seems to work best. If you give more than this, people have difficulty making distinctions.

One issue you'll have to deal with is "tie votes"—do you want to allow them or not? Most researchers do not like ties; they make statistical analyses more complicated. You will have to include instructions that make it clear that no ties are allowed. The other critical issue is leaving out an important reason. You definitely do not want people adding to the list because respondents would be ranking different lists, making it harder to compare across your sample.

When formatting this type of question, there is a temptation to use a variation of the open-ended question response format. You could list the seven things to be ranked and then put a line at the end of each with an instruction to "put a 1 by your most important, a 2 by your next most important reason. . . . " This might work all right, but again you are risking illegible handwriting. One way out is to list the possible rankings opposite each item and ask the respondent to circle their response.

Ranking

a. item A: 1st   2nd   3rd   4th   5th   6th   7th
b. item B: 1st   2nd   3rd   4th   5th   6th   7th

Rating Scales

RATING scales are a very common type of item used in questionnaires. The form of a rating scale is to include a list of alternatives that range from not much of a particular attribute to a great deal of that same attribute, for example: Excellent, Very Good, Good, Fair, or Poor. One particular subset of rating scales is the LIKERT (lick-ert) scale. These include degrees of "agreement" and "disagreement."

Strongly	Agree	Unsure	Disagree	Strongly
Agree				Disagree

When one tries to construct a rating scale, there are several factors one must consider. We'll discuss each in turn.

Psychological Distance. Ideally, your scale points will be selected such that respondents interpret the "distance" between each pair of points to be equal. For the most part this is done subjectively, the key concern being that you do not want huge gaps in your scale or two adjacent points being almost synonymous. Below are some examples of scales that have problems.

Excellent	Very Good	. . .	Fair	Poor	(big gap)
Excellent	. . .	Good	Average	Fair	Poor	(points too close)
Excellent	Very Good	. . .	. . .	Poor	(big gap)

The Number of Response Alternatives. Commonly we see items with between 3 and 7 scale points. Sometimes we see 10 points or 100 points. Very infrequently we see something else. How do you choose between 3 and 7 points or something else? The answer will depend on your particular study and the analyses you want to do. In general, you want to give people enough categories so that they can represent their feelings or experiences, but not so many that you are asking them to make inconsequential distinctions. Other than avoiding too many categories, there is no overwhelming reason to pick a certain number of categories over another.

The Order of Presentation of Categories. The categories should be displayed in a way that is monotonically increasing or decreasing. This means the categories are typed in a horizontal row or are presented in a vertical list. They should not be typed in a way that is ambiguous as to the order. This circumstance can arise when you type the alternatives on two lines like this:

| Excellent | Very Good |
| Good | Fair |

It is probably good to mix up your presentation within the questionnaire such that sometimes you will have monotonically increasing items and sometimes decreasing. You should *not* do this within a group of items measuring a particular issue, but rather on different pages dealing with different issues. By doing this, you will present respondents with one format for a particular issue but keep them "on their toes" if you do some switching of formats from section to section.

Unipolar or Bipolar Scales. This issue relates to whether the choice of words for your categories ranges from "nothing" to "a great deal" (unipolar) *or* ranges from "a large negative rating" through "zero" and then to "a large positive rating" (bipolar). For example:

Unipolar:	Excellent	Very Good	Good	Fair	Poor
Bipolar:	Strongly Disagree	Disagree	Unsure	Agree	Strongly Agree

Again, there is really no reason to choose one format over another other than personal preference or the dictates of your analysis plans.

Odd Versus Even Numbers of Choices. There is only one aspect that makes a difference between choosing even numbers versus odd numbers of choices. If you choose an odd number you create a natural middle point; this is obvious in the bipolar example above; the "unsure" response is in the middle of agree and disagree. Even in the unipolar example the "good" category becomes the "middle." You could strengthen this association for that particular scale if you revised it to read:

Excellent   Very Good   Average   Fair   Poor.

The question then becomes, do you want a middle point? On a unipolar scale it hardly matters either way—four versus five versus six points would not make a great difference in the form of the data. Use what you feel comfortable with and that which seems to fit your topic. On a bipolar scale the issue takes on more significance. The reason is that if you give people a middle choice they will use it. For the analysis of some questions this would be fine; in other instances you may want to "force" respondents to choose which side of the fence they are on. In that case you may not want to give respondents the option of selecting a middle point. If you are asking respondents to make tough choices by agreeing or disagreeing with a complex, emotional issue you may want to help them make fine distinctions by using a six-point scale with the "middle two" categories being "close" to the middle. For example:

Strongly Disagree	Disagree	Slightly Disagree	Slightly Agree	Agree	Strongly Agree

Balanced Scales. One of the sure signs of a poorly designed survey is a question that has an unbalanced scale. An unbalanced scale is created when the number of points above and below the "middle" of the scale are uneven.

Strongly Agree	Agree	Slightly Agree	(Unlabeled middle)	Disagree

Why is this such a problem? Basically you are biasing your answers in one direction or the other. In the above example, respondents had three chances to "agree" and only one chance to "disagree." If a study used such a scale, it wouldn't be surprising to see results that said: "Nearly 80% of the city's population agrees that the mayor is doing a good job." It may be that they really feel that way; on the other hand it could merely be an artifact of the way the scale was constructed.

Presenting a "Don't Know" Category. Should you present a "don't know" category in your list of responses? If you present it, more respondents will use it than if you do not. On the other hand, respondents may be irritated if that is what they want to say, and there is no easy way to express this response. Certainly when you are asking knowledge type questions, you should provide a "don't know" response. It is useful to know how many "don't know." When you are asking attitudinal questions, the "don't know" sometimes is equivalent to no opinion, but sometimes it means "I've got mixed feelings about the issue." My experience is that when questions ask only do you "agree" or "disagree," people are reluctant to take such an all or nothing stand, and that is when they look for the "don't know." One solution is to offer more categories closer to the middle, so that it is easier to capture persons who are "leaning" one way or the other.

Converse and Presser (1986) suggest asking first whether people have an opinion, and then if they do to ask what it is. I think this is possible to do in a mail survey, but it is somewhat cumbersome and puts additional instructions in the flow of the questions. You have to consider how many people really "don't know" and how useful it is for you to have this information explicitly.

Behaviorally Anchored Scales. There are two types of phrases that can be used to describe your scale points: You can use subjective terms (e.g., a lot, some, a few) or you can use behaviorally anchored terms (e.g., more than 5 times, 3 to 4 times, 1 to 2 times). The advantage in using behaviorally anchored scales is that you are more certain that people mean the same thing when they give the same answer. For instance, when asking two supervisors how often their employees come in late, both might say "a lot." However, in reality one may mean 10 times or more, whereas the other might mean 3 or 4 times. By using a behaviorally anchored scale, this difference in the real situation would become known.

Why, then, would anyone use subjectively worded terms? For some questions you really want to know how respondents evaluate an issue, not just have them report the objective reality. In these circumstances, a subjectively worded scale is better. In our example above with the two supervisors, although they have groups of employees who are late at different rates, both feel that it is "a lot," and this is an important piece of information. The choice of which type of scale is more appropriate for you must be based on the analytic goals of your questions.

GUIDELINES FOR THE CONTENT OF QUESTIONS

Obviously I cannot give you a cookbook recipe for wording each of your questions. Every study is different; each topic could be explored somewhat differently given your interests and the study's goals. What I can give you are some guidelines that will help you write high quality questions.

What is our basic goal in writing a question? We want to create a question that provides a standardized stimulus to all respondents and provides a systematic way of recording their answers. By paying attention to the guidelines outlined below, you will be able to write questions that will meet this overall question design objective.

Before we get into specifics, there are a few principles to keep in mind about the question writing process.

1. In order to write a question you need a *specific* goal for each item. The goal has to be so specific that any of your colleagues could write a question from this specified goal and you would recognize it as meeting your objective. (It might not be worded exactly as you would word it, but it should measure the same aspect.) For example, this is *not* a specific enough question goal: "I want to know how people feel about their jobs." This may be a goal for a study or a part of a questionnaire, but you cannot write a question from it because the goal is too abstract. We *could* write a question from this goal: "I want to know how satisfied people are with the financial rewards of their job."

   One of the best ways to develop these specific goals is to outline your questionnaire before you write any items. First, divide your survey into five or six broad topic areas (e.g., demographics, characteristics of the job, family responsibilities, personality measures, life satisfactions). Then break each of those areas down into specific issues you want to explore. Within each of these issues, specify the particular aspects you want to measure. When you have this outline completed, the most detailed part of the outline should correspond to an item in your survey. From this point it is only a matter of wrestling with the exact wording.

2. You also need a few guidelines and rules to follow as you create questions. These will be provided in the remainder of this chapter.

3. You need common sense. Unfortunately this is sometimes negatively correlated with education, and often a survey author has quite a bit of education. You need to design questions that make sense to the average person.

4. You need to develop the ability to get "outside the question" and "hear" it from a naive perspective. Unfortunately, this ability is negatively correlated with involvement in the authorship of the questions. However, to be a good critic, to assess whether the question as currently worded is going to adequately serve your needs, you really need to read the question not as an author (who knows its intent) but as someone reading it for the first time. This way you can "hear" the problems, or "see" the flaws in the wording.

So what are the guidelines to follow in constructing a question?

1. Write Brief Questions

I do not recommend this just because I want to save paper. Brief questions are more valid questions because they are more likely to be read completely, less likely to have qualifying phrases, and less susceptible to extraneous influences on the respondents' answers (Armstrong & Overton, 1971). In particular, they are less susceptible to biases produced by format or positioning of the response alternatives.

One of the ways that people get into trouble and write overly long questions is that they use extraneous words or phrases that take up space but do not add anything essential to the question. Another reason is that authors want to put many qualifiers into their question. Finally, authors try to get too much out of a single question. Here is an example of an *unbrief* question:

> "If you combine the value of all your (and members of your family living here) savings and investments such as savings and checking accounts, the cash value of your life insurance, stocks, bonds, and things like that, plus what you would keep if you sold your real estate, including your home, which of the categories below comes closest to your total assets?"

There are really two ways to improve this question. The first is to make it simpler without all the qualifiers, and therefore settle for an answer that is "close enough but not perfect." If you really need all the details, another approach is to break the question up into its component parts, each of which can be made into a relatively simple question.

2. Write Clear Questions

Nobody purposely writes unclear questions, but sometimes people are so close to the topic and know so well what they intend that they just do not realize how convoluted they have made things. There are a variety of methods that can help you write clearer questions.

a. Define Key Terms

Within the question itself, you can define a key term, particularly if it is subject to alternate meanings. If you are going to define a term, the definition should come at the *beginning* of the question. For instance:

> "How do you feel about the amount you pay the government on the money you take in during the year, that is, your income tax?"

b. Beware of Expert Jargon

You have to be extremely cautious about using terms that are common in your field but may not be readily understood by the average person. In a health study I worked on the clients wanted to ask mothers how many *prenatal* visits they had. The researchers knew exactly what "prenatal" meant, but we convinced them that they needed to define the term so that mothers would not be confused about what we meant.

c. Beware of Unclear Referents of Pronouns

This problem arises frequently when you are doing a series of questions about a particular topic and you start using "it" and "they." A close reading of the questions might show you that it is not clear what "it" refers to.

d. Avoid Double Negatives

Usually a question can be reworded to avoid a double negative construction. Sometimes such constructions are hard to avoid because the referent of the question has a negative connotation, for example, "Do you agree or disagree that the current seat belt law should be repealed?" Usually, these types of questions can be reworded to make them simpler to understand. For example, "Do you think there should be a mandatory seat belt use law, or do you think we should not have such a law?"

e. Avoid Adverbial Question Constructions

Avoid adverbial question constructions. Avoid wording that starts with "how," "why," "when," "where," or "how much." These terms are inherently ambiguous although you think you are being perfectly clear. For example:

"WHERE do you live?" Do you mean address, town, or type of building?

"WHEN did you go to that school?" Do you mean what year, how many years ago, or how old were you when you did?

In a self-administered format in which you provide the answer categories, this issue may not be a tremendous problem, but if you are using open-ended formats, you may be surprised at the types of answers people write down.

3. Stay in Touch With Reality

When you write your questions, be aware of "reality" issues and how they might affect your data. In particular, there are four issues to consider.

a. Intention Questions

If you write a question asking about someone's intentions, you should understand that the answers may not reflect actual future behavior. At best, intentions should be viewed as an attitude. Sometimes attitudes correspond to behavior and sometimes they do not. Sometimes our future behavior is different from an earlier stated intention because of intervening events. When pollsters ask people whom they intend to vote for for president, they have a better chance of predicting the election if they calculate the responses only for those people who are more likely to actually go to the polls (e.g., registered voters or people who voted in the last election).

b. Hypothetical Questions

These questions are difficult ones to answer in general because everybody says "it depends." Make sure that all parts of the question are included in the hypothetical.

For example:

> "If a friend of yours were looking for a job, would you recommend your employer?" Answer: "No, because there are no openings."

Instead the question should read:

> "If your employer had an opening and if a friend . . ."

I have found that hypotheticals are particularly hard for people with high intelligence and those with lower intelligence. The high IQ people see all the contingencies and therefore cannot take a stand, whereas the lower IQ people cannot imagine the circumstance you posit.

c. Ask Only Relevant Questions

A series of questions may not be relevant for a particular group of respondents. For instance, if you have a series of questions on pregnancy care, you want the males to skip over them, or if you have a series of questions about spousal interactions, you want the unmarried to skip over these. You want to use some kind of screening question at the beginning of a sequence to decide who should continue and who should skip. You also want to make sure your instructions are clear about who should go where in the questionnaire.

d. Commonplace Is Not Universal

Not everyone has only one job; the self-employed may not have "income." Beware particularly of the rich and such responses as "But I don't shop, the housekeeper does" and "House? Which one?" The sequence of questions you ask and the format of the answer categories needs to anticipate such circumstances.

4. Write Unidimensional Questions

A unidimensional question has one issue that it addresses. Avoid double- (or triple-) barreled questions. In other words, do not combine two or three questions within one question. Again, for the most part people do not purposely do this; they fall into it as they try to make the question clearer. The tipoff to a problem question is usually the word "and" or "or." For example:

"How friendly *and* helpful are your coworkers?"

The problem with this question is that some coworkers may be friendly but not helpful or helpful but not friendly. Another example that is not quite so obvious:

"Do you think personal income taxes should be lowered by 4% in order to help the economy?"

This is actually three questions. Should income taxes be lowered? Should they be lowered by 4%? Will this help the economy? The solution is always easy: Break the question up into its component questions or rewrite it to focus on the issue you really are interested in.

5. Write Mutually Exclusive Response Categories

One common problem in draft questions is that answer alternatives overlap. Sometimes the overlap comes because the author has been sloppy with his or her alternatives. Sometimes it is just laziness: It is easier to write categories that end in round numbers (e.g., age categories 25-30, 30-35, 35-40, etc.). The issue is, of course, the people whose answer corresponds to the endpoint—they do not know which category to check. Marital status is another example of this type of problem— "married, single, widowed, divorced, or separated." The "single" category overlaps with widowed, divorced, and separated. Using "never married" solves this problem.

6. Create Exhaustive Response Categories

It should almost go without saying that you want to provide response choices that reflect almost everybody's position and therefore you need to consider the whole range of answers that someone might give. There are two situations that commonly occur that create problems. One is with scales in which there are uneven aspects to the distance between points on your scale, and so "psychologically" (for subjective scales) or "objectively" (for behavioral scales) there is an answer "missing." A closely related issue is endpoints that are not strictly parallel. For example:

Always   Often   Sometimes   Rarely

The "rarely" response is not parallel to the "always" response; what is missing is the "never" choice.

The second situation involves questions where you are giving "reasons" as choices and you leave out the favorite answer of a large segment of your sample. As I will discuss later in this chapter, there are some fairly straightforward ways to spot these problems.

7. Do Not Write Loaded Questions

A loaded question is a biased or slanted question. It is written in such a way as to "force" people to answer in one direction or another. Unfortunately, there are many examples of this problem. Often the "researchers" have purposes in mind other than discovering truth. For example:

> "Should the state ignore the principles of the Bible, which is the law of God, and morality by legalizing murder by abortion?"

Often the loading happens in a more subtle fashion. We have discussed earlier how writing scales that are not balanced stacks the deck toward one end or the other. In addition, loading happens because particular words or phrases are used that invoke strong positive or strong negative reactions (e.g., American institution, giveaway programs). Also, invoking authority figures within the question can bias responses (e.g., God, the Supreme Court, the president). Even invoking the status quo can slant responses. For example:

> "Up until now gambling has been illegal in this state. How do you feel about legalizing gambling?"

Finally, another phrasing that biases answers is to use social pressure within a question.

> "In the last election a large majority rejected proposition X. How do you feel about it now?"

or

> "Most people feel that smoking marijuana is harmful. How do you feel?"

In all these situations, the loading or biasing can be removed relatively easily by writing a question from a neutral stance. What you want to do is to give both sides of the issue, or both ends of the scale, an equal presentation. Mostly this can be achieved by writing the question without adding the various strategies listed above. Sometimes what you need to do is be explicit about both sides. For example:

> "Some people support legalized gambling, others want it to be illegal; how do you feel about it?" (As an aside to the reader, when I first typed this example I wrote ". . . others want it to *remain* illegal." It is very easy to slip and write a loaded question; in this case using the status quo in my first wording.)

I do not want to end this discussion without making one point about phrasings that use social pressure. In one circumstance an argument can be made that it will make your data more valid. There are behaviors or attitudes that people might really do or hold but because of a social stigma they would be reluctant to admit to it. By using a loaded structure in your question you try to counterbalance this force and free people to report honestly. For example:

"Most people have times when they drink too much and feel tipsy. How often has that happened to you in the past month?"

Obviously, the use of such procedures must be done carefully and be based on previous results that show that there is a social norm operating to inhibit responses. As we will see in chapters to follow, there are other ways within the structure of the questionnaire to free people to be honest, and these strategies should be considered as well.

HOW TO CREATE QUESTIONS

Even with these guidelines, it is still a significant task to produce a series of questions. There are several ways in which the question producing process can work well. When we talk about developing questions, we assume that you have a fairly good idea of the issues that need to be explored. However, how does one get that fairly good idea?

Having a command of prior work in the field is a tremendous boost to creating a new questionnaire. Reviewing prior studies will help you develop a model for understanding your research area. It will also help you identify the unknown areas or the ones in which confusing findings have been reported. This will help you identify the most fertile ground for your explorations.

Besides prior research, exploratory efforts can help you map out the terrain. These exploratory efforts might consist of relatively unstructured interviews with a small number of people who represent a mix of circumstances, or they might represent interviews with knowledgeable observers of the issues you want to research. For instance, you might talk with doctors and nurses about their views on what makes for quick recoveries after surgical procedures.

In addition to these techniques, focus groups are a wonderful mechanism to help you understand the important issues that relate to your topic of study. A focus group is like a group interview with a small number of persons (maybe 6 to 12). The idea is to get the group to focus on an issue and to discuss their perspectives and experiences. A synergism exists in the group dynamic when one member hears what another member is reporting. Sometimes there is sharp disagreement and sometimes widespread agreement. It is up to the leader of the group to make sure the group follows a productive process including giving everyone a chance to be heard, making it clear that the purpose is to hear where people agree or differ, and to guide the discussion to various broad areas. You may want to tape these meetings and then extract issues by listening again to the tape, or you might want to have a colleague sit in with you to take copious notes. What the focus group is good at is identifying issues; it cannot really tell you how many people feel one way and how many feel another—that is for your survey.

Pretests

No researcher ever created a perfect survey with the first draft. Getting to the final version of your questions and your questionnaire takes many rounds of revisions. Each time you revise a question, it should get better. To make your revisions effective, however, you need to have information that tells you what you need to revise.

First, you can do a lot yourself just by giving your questions a critical reading. Remember my advice about "hearing" your questions from a naive perspective. This is where this skill comes in handy. As you critically assess your questions, keep in mind what your analytic objectives are. What kind of information do you really want to get?

Second, you can get a lot of feedback from colleagues. Some will be more enthusiastic than others about telling you where you have gone wrong, but try to stay nondefensive and hear what the problem is that they are having with it. Do not rush too quickly to say, "Oh you misunderstood what I was trying to get at . . . " If they misunderstood, maybe a respondent would also.

Third, you can try some informal data gathering by using willing students, or friends for whom the opportunity to fill out the questionnaire on this topic might be interesting. Get feedback from them on the length of time it took, places where it was confusing, and things you might have left out.

Fourth, you are ready for your first formal pretesting of your questionnaire. Some authors suggest trying out all of your procedures on a small scale, including your introductory letter and your data collection phases (Sletto, 1940)—a pilot test. There is nothing wrong with testing out your procedures, but you need more information than merely how quickly the questionnaires come back and what they look like when they are returned. The critical issue is that you want feedback on the questions themselves.

What you want to do, although your real procedure will be a mail survey, is to gather in a room about 10 individuals who represent the kind of person who will be in your sample. Preferably they will not know you. You can recruit these people through colleagues, through a continuing education course at a local junior college, or through direct recruiting via the phone by you or your research assistant. Depending on whether they have to come to you or not, you may want to pay them a small stipend ($10-$25), and you at least want to provide coffee and doughnuts (maybe fruit if this is a health survey).

People generally like to be helpful. Tell them at the beginning that you want to get a good estimate of the time it takes to fill out the questionnaire and that you need feedback on unclear instructions, ambiguous wording, confusing questions, questions that are too difficult to answer, and questions that they do not like answering. Let everybody finish (remind them to record start and end times) and then move to a discussion about the questionnaire. First get overall feedback—did they enjoy it or not, how was the length, did they like the way the survey looked, was it easy to read? Then move on to specific sections of the questionnaire. Go through it page by page, asking for any issues that they might have had. Sometimes pretest respondents are reluctant to criticize; after all, you are the expert, and what do they know about research? It is up to you to make them feel at ease and to encourage them to help you work out the "kinks" in the survey. Make them feel a part of the process. Sometimes you can get them talking by asking them if they think "others" might have problems understanding any of the questions. You should also ask them if you have left out issues within each section that they think would be important to know. This is somewhat like the focus group process, but with a specific stimulus. You should run enough groups so that you have at least 25 pretests; more would be better.

In addition to obtaining reactions from your pretest respondents, you may also want to specifically ask them what their reasoning was when they checked a specific box or what definition they applied to a critical term. In a recent study, we used the term "work group" in a study of job factors and health. We wanted to know whether respondents' notions of work group corresponded to ours. We discovered that respondents have different definitions, so we added our definition to the wording of the question. This process provides a wealth of feedback on the understanding of key terms and the processes that respondents use to formulate answers. All of this information is useful in determining whether you need to revise items and how to revise them so that they are better able to assess your question objectives.

Besides the feedback from the respondents, you should tabulate their answers and look at the distributions that you get. Also note how many people refused to answer questions or left them blank. You should be suspicious of items on which everybody is answering the same thing or almost the same thing. These kinds of items will not be very useful in any kind of comparative analysis. You have to ask yourself if you expect people to vary on this item. If yes, then why are you not getting that variation? Is the item loaded? Are the response categories not balanced? Maybe you need more gradations where the bulge of responses is. If you do not expect variation, then you might ask yourself if you really need this item.

Inevitably, your questionnaire will be too long, *and* you will think of additional items that you want to add based on the group's feedback. A good researcher can always think of additional interesting questions to ask. Here is where discipline comes in: You really need to stick with your analytic objectives and not try to do everything in one study. Cut out the nonessential questions, trim back on the second priority areas, and add in some of the additional ideas. Revise wording, question ordering, and formats.

Then pretest a second time! You may feel that you do not have time or resources, or you may feel that the revisions you made will work, so you might be tempted to skip the second pretest. Don't. It is worth the time and effort. Your study will be significantly better from doing a second pretest. What you have to tell yourself is that it is not worth the real study turning out to be just a big second pretest. You will regret your shortcuts when it comes time to write up the results.

In stressing two pretests, I do not mean to imply that you never do more. Sometimes you do many. It depends on how much development work you are doing, and it depends on how complicated the material is and how broad it is. Sometimes you only pretest sections of the questionnaire. I do not recall ever hearing a researcher say that the time spent in pretesting was a waste. I do recall many researchers saying, "I only wished I had pretested more."

3

Question Design: The Advanced Course

In the last chapter we went over the basics of question design. In this chapter we want to focus on a few issues in more depth. These considerations will move your questions from good questions to superb questions.

ITEM NONRESPONSE

It is really discouraging for you to get your questionnaires back and find questions that were left blank or refused, or answers given in the margins that are alternatives to the ones you presented. In most of these cases, the information is lost forever, and there is nothing to do but to accept the fact that you have incomplete data. With luck, for any one question the proportion not providing usable information will be small. If there are many missing responses, you can hope that they are not on a crucial variable.

The only real solution to this problem is at the question design stage. Your pretests may have indicated items that were having nonresponse problems so that you were able to fix the problems before sending out your survey.

Why do people not respond to items? (See Adams, 1956; Craig & McCann, 1978.) Sometimes it is because the item is not relevant to the individual. Questions about school quality or kids' recreation opportunities might be skipped by respondents without children. The solution here is to use some kind of contingency question with a skip instruction. We will deal with this below.

Sometimes respondents skip an item because it is confusing or they do not understand what is wanted from them. Pretesting should pick up these problems. Revision requires simpler language, providing a definition, or breaking up a question into subparts.

I have also found that respondents leave questions blank or provide their own answers when you give them too few categories and they do

not feel their position is represented. This is particularly true for attitudinal items that have a lot of emotional complexity to them (e.g., items
about abortion, or capital punishment, or trade barriers with Japan).
Instead of just an agree-disagree format, use four categories, or even
six. This allows people in the middle to express which side they are
leaning toward.

For items that are more factual, missing answers imply that people
"don't know." If this problem occurs often in your pretesting, then you
should probably provide a "don't know" response.

SCREENING QUESTIONS AND SKIP INSTRUCTIONS

There are two occasions when you want respondents to skip over a
sequence of questions. First, they might provide an answer that indi-
cates that the subsequent sequence of questions, which gather greater
detail, is not applicable to them. For example, people who say they have
not looked for a job in the past month do not need to answer questions
about where they looked or how many interviews they have had. Second, they might have a demographic characteristic that makes the series
irrelevant to them, for example, asking a series of questions on pregnancy experiences to a woman who has never been pregnant or questions on college experiences to those who did not attend college.

Conceptually, it is relatively easy to provide instructions to tell some
people to skip over a sequence and go to the next appropriate question.
In practice, this turns out to be more difficult than it seems. You need
to make your directions explicit. Do not assume the respondent can
figure it out. You need to make your instructions clear for both groups,
those who should continue and those who should skip. You need to
facilitate your instructions by visual aides such as arrows, boxes, or bold
type. Try to have people skip to somewhere else on the same page, or
if you have to send them to another page, try to put the next question at
the top of that page. The example in Figure 3.1 shows a page from a
questionnaire in which the instructions are clear.

MULTIPLE QUESTIONS AND RELIABILITY

Reliability is the property of a question that allows it to consistently
give you the same answer in similar circumstances. When we think of

G12. About how much did you weigh when you were 18 years old?

　　　　＿＿＿＿＿ Pounds

G13. Are you now trying to lose weight?

　　　　　　1 ☐　Yes　　　　　2 ☐　No ━━━━━━▶GO TO G16

┌───┐
│ G14. Are you eating fewer calories to lose weight?   │
│   1 ☐　Yes　　　　　2 ☐　No   │
│   │
│ G15. Have you increased your physical activity to lose weight?│
│   1 ☐　Yes　　　　　2 ☐　No   │
└───┘

G16. Do you consider yourself to be ..(Check one)

　　　　　1 ☐　Very overweight
　　　　　2 ☐　Somewhat overweight
　　　　　3 ☐　A little overweight
　　　　　4 ☐　About the right weight
　　　　　5 ☐　Underweight

G17. On average, how many cups of coffee do you drink a day?

　　　　　0 ☐　None ━━━━━▶GO TO G19
　　　　＿＿＿＿＿ No. of cups

┌───┐
│ G18. Is the coffee you usually drink decaffeinated or regular coffee? (Check one) │
│   1 ☐　Decaffeinated   │
│   2 ☐　Regular   │
│   3 ☐　About half of each   │
└───┘

G19. On average, how many cups of tea, either hot or iced, do you drink a day?

　　　　　0 ☐　None
　　　　＿＿＿＿＿ No. of cups

Figure 3.1. An Example of Clear Instructions

error in measurement, we are concerned about minimizing random error that makes our questions inconsistent—either inconsistent over time or inconsistent across measures of similar concepts.

One of the ways to improve the reliability of measurement of a particular concept is to include in your survey more than one question that measures the concept and then to average the responses to the multiple questions. Why does this work to reduce random measurement error? Random error is just what its name implies—random. For no predictable reason, an answer recorded may not be a "true" answer for the respondent. The answer given may be a little too high or a little too low, but randomly so. Maybe somebody accidentally checked the wrong box, or they got confused about the order of the categories.

By having multiple questions asking about the same concept, random errors are overcome. It is very unlikely, for instance, that two items would both have the same random error at the same time. So by taking the average of the two, we will be closer to the true answer than we would have been if we had only taken the one item with its random error. Both items may have error, but they are likely to cancel each other out because the error they contain was from a random source. This cancelling of error process is more likely to be the case as the number of alternate questions measuring the same concept increases.

Now when we say multiple items, we do not mean five items that are essentially the same item with slight tense changes or other minor phrasing differences. Instead, we are talking about a small group of items that get at the same basic concept but from somewhat different angles or somewhat different components. For instance, if I want to measure a respondent's satisfaction with his or her financial rewards at work I might include items on his or her pay level, sense of pay equity, frequency of cost of living adjustments, fringe benefits, and pay increase expectations. By putting all these together into an average response, I am much more likely to measure financial rewards' satisfaction reliably.

IMPROVING QUALITY OF
DATA FOR SENSITIVE QUESTIONS

There are two reasons why sensitive items might produce poorer quality data: People may forget unpleasant thoughts and people like to portray themselves in a good light. We will talk about solutions to "forgetting" later in this chapter. Here we will deal with looking desirable. Obviously people like to look good; they do not like to admit that they have weaknesses such as drunk driving, buying pornography, having unprotected sex outside a monogamous relationship, not voting in elections, not going to the dentist twice a year, and so on. The challenge for you then is to write a question that helps people respond with answers that are close to the truth even though the truth may not be socially desirable.

First, decide if you really need this kind of information for your study purposes. Only ask sensitive questions that are necessary. Closely related to this consideration is to ask yourself how much detail you really need about this issue. Asking people how often they used cocaine or marijuana in the past month is different from asking people if they "ever" tried cocaine or marijuana. Do not ask for extra details if you do not need them.

Second, when creating your categories, also think of what is the least amount of detail that you need. By making a sensitive question also a difficult question, you risk even greater refusals. For instance, if you want to ask about family income, do you really need to know an exact figure? Remember the last time you filled out your IRS Form 1040; sometimes it is hard to come up with an accurate, exact figure even in this situation, and that is even with all those W-2 forms available. Even if you are using categories, ask yourself, can you get by with larger ranges on your categories (e.g., $20,000 to $40,000 rather than $20,000 to $25,000)? The fewer the categories (and therefore the broader the ranges) the fewer missing answers you will get for sensitive, factual items.

Third, only ask the question of people for whom it is directly relevant. In some of our AIDS surveys, we wanted to know how many persons had unprotected anal sex. As we thought about this question and why we needed to ask it, it became clearer that this was a "risk" factor only for individuals who had other risk factors (e.g., IV drug users, people with multiple partners, etc.) and it was not really a risk factor for those who were in long-term, monogamous relationships. Therefore, we decided to ask the question only of people for whom it was relevant to find out their answer.

Fourth, if the purpose of the question seems arbitrary, this will cause problems. Some of the most sensitive questions turn out to be those that ask about people's income. In the abstract, respondents feel it is none of our business, but although most people are not researchers, they can understand why a researcher might want to compare groups of people who are in different situations. Sometimes, therefore, an introduction to a section of demographic questions telling respondents why you need this information can help.

Fifth, the context within which you ask the question can help you. To continue with the example about the income question, most researchers include income along with the rest of the demographic questions at the end of the questionnaire. We had occasion in a survey to ask, in the middle of the questionnaire, a whole series of questions about financial circumstances and how things had either improved or gotten worse for the respondent. We also asked the respondents to tell us how satisfied they were with their income. Within this context, we then asked what their current income was. Respondents could easily grasp why we needed to know their current income in the light of the other questions. We had very few missing answers to the income question on that survey.

Sixth, helping respondents feel that their answer is not that "odd" will reduce distortion. There are several ways to accomplish that. If you are asking about frequency of the behavior, have the end of your scale represented by a term that means "really often." Those who just do it "often" will not feel that their answer is way up there. You can suggest that some people do this kind of behavior as an introduction. You can precede your key question with a couple of questions that get into the topic and that help set the tone that others are engaging in the behavior. We used this strategy when asking teenagers how often they drank alcohol. We first asked what proportion of their friends had a drink of alcohol at least once in the past month (a cut-point that would include quite a few teenagers). Many teens said "most" or "about half" of their friends did so. Then we asked them how often they drank in the past month. Now they were answering this question within the context of just telling us that "many" of their friends drank too. It therefore made them more at ease in reporting their own behavior.

QUESTION ORDER EFFECTS

Question order effects refer to the finding that the answers to a particular question may depend on its sequencing in the questionnaire. In other words, the answers to a question are dependent on the questions that precede it. Research has shown order effects for interviewer-based methodologies (Bishop, Oldendick, & Tuchfarber, 1984; Schuman, Kalton, & Ludwig, 1983; Schuman & Presser, 1981; Schuman & Scott, 1987). There are, however, research findings that show that this problem is not as great when using mail survey strategies (Ayidiya & McClendon, 1990; Bishop et al., 1984). The explanation for this difference is that in mail surveys the respondents can look at all the items before they answer or easily go back and change answers at any point;

therefore, the answers are not necessarily the result of a single order of answering the questions. In contrast, the interviewer-administered questions are usually given in the same order, with little opportunity to go back and switch answers.

RESPONSE ORDER EFFECTS

Response order effects arise because of the order in which the response alternatives are given. Two types of order effects have been identified: recency effects, which means more often choosing the last category offered, and primacy effects, which means more often choosing the first category offered. Recency effects are a particular problem in interviewer-administered surveys (Schuman & Presser, 1981). The studies by Ayidiya and McClendon (1990) and Bishop et al. (1984) provide evidence that recency effects are much less of an issue in self-administered surveys. Again, the presumption is that respondents can read and reread the alternate categories offered; therefore, the order in which they are presented should make little difference.

RESPONSE SET BIASES

A response set bias is a factor that operates to produce a particular pattern of answers that may not exactly correspond to the true state of affairs. There are several types of response set biases that you should be aware of when designing your questions.

Acquiescence Bias

This is the tendency to say "yes" or to act "agreeable." The easiest way to deal with this bias is to write the stems of your questions such that some are "reversed." This will cause people who want to be consistent with their viewpoint to have to answer some questions "yes" and some "no." Forcing respondents to break the set of always answering "yes" will make you more confident of their answers. I also believe that having more scale points rather than just yes-no or agree- disagree will force respondents to consider the fine points of their attitudes and not just go down the page saying "yes," "yes."

Beginning-Ending List Bias

This is a tendency to pick items at the beginning or end of long lists. Many people do not read the whole list or, if they do, they remember the items listed last. The easiest way to deal with this is not to give long lists of choices. If you really must have all the choices considered, then you could break them up into a couple of shorter subgroups of alternatives or you could turn them into a series of yes-no questions. In this way the respondents have to consider each item.

Central Tendency Bias

This is the tendency to answer in the middle, to look average. There are two ways to overcome this tendency. One is to increase the range of your choices so that the ones near the center are the ones you are most interested in. Another way is to leave out the middle response. If you do this, however, you need to leave categories that are close to both sides of the middle so that respondents can easily say which way they are leaning.

All these response set biases operate more severely when the question itself is not clear. If respondents cannot figure out what you mean by the question, then they are more apt to be influenced in their answers by one of these response set biases.

Recall Bias

Overcoming recall bias, the tendency to forget or to misremember particular information, is at the heart of quality survey methodology. A detailed description of these issues is contained in a chapter by Nancy Mathiowetz in Biemer et al. (1991).

Recall bias occurs because our memories are not perfect recordings of everything that has happened to us. Our memories are "saved" in ways that are not letter-perfect reproductions of our experiences, and our "recall" mechanisms are subject to distortions.

One factor that affects our memory and is perhaps the easiest to understand is the length of the recall period. The longer ago something happened, the more likely we are to forget it or to distort it, all else being equal. In particular we may have "recall decay," the inability to remember "it" at all. We may also experience "telescoping error," which is misremembering the exact period in which the event happened and instead giving an answer that is either too early or too late.

The obvious solution is to limit your questions to shorter recall periods. Instead of "ever," use "last year" or "last month" or "last week" or "yesterday." The only problem with shorter recall periods is that you will get fewer behaviors reported because the period is shorter (although it will be a more accurate reporting). If your study requires asking further information about these behaviors, you will want to have as many behaviors as possible to investigate. Therefore, there is a tendency to use a longer period to get more "reports." The choice of the length of your recall period should provide a balance between quality of memory and amount of information available to be reported.

How important an issue is to a person also affects the ability to remember. If an event is minor, then it is easily forgotten. Major events, such as surgical operations, marriages, deaths, and job changes, are more impervious to forgetting. Again, the primary solution is to consider the period when constructing these questions. If you are asking about major events, then you can get away with a longer recall period; for minor events (e.g., how many cups of coffee you had), it is best to keep the recall period short.

Another aspect that affects memory is the regularity of the behavior. If someone "always" has a martini before dinner and a glass of wine with dinner, and that is the only time they drink, then it is easy for them to recall how much they drink in a day, or a week, or a month, or even in a year. Events that are irregular are more difficult to recall and therefore require more careful consideration of the question wording.

Besides shortening the recall period, there are other strategies that can aid in recall. For instance, providing a list of medical conditions and asking people whether they had these conditions is a more accurate strategy than asking generally whether they have had any medical conditions and, if so, asking what they were.

Using a boundary to a recall period that is a notable date, such as January 1 or the respondent's birthday, or since the beginning of school for parents with children, helps people to accurately recall information because they have a marker in their memories that helps organize the information that is stored in their brain.

Another strategy that is helpful is to recreate the mood, or the situation in which the events took place, to help with recall. To get an idea of how this works, think for yourself how much more easily you can recall things about your childhood when you go back to your parents' home for a visit compared to trying to remember incidents or details when you are not at your childhood home. If you wanted to ask about incidents during a person's childhood, you could use this device by asking the respondent to "think back to the time when you were growing up in your parents' home ... back then how often did you ... "

A final suggestion about aiding recall has to do with the organization of your questionnaire.

FLOW OF THE QUESTIONNAIRE

There are lots of benefits to having the right order or flow of questions in your questionnaire. Respondents find it easier to use the questionnaire and enjoy filling it out. A questionnaire with good flow also helps them to remember more accurately and makes them more willing to provide accurate information.

Three guidelines are important to keep in mind when you start making decisions about how to put your questions together into an effective questionnaire. One is putting questions together that make sense to ask together, the second is to order the questions logically within a section, and the third is not to start or end with your hardest questions.

Grouping questions into subtopics helps respondents keep a frame of reference as they answer the questions. For instance, ask all your questions about their job in one section, all the marriage and family questions in another section, their housing questions in another section, and their neighborhood services questions in still another section. It sometimes gets tricky when you are asking about two different periods (e.g., now and 5 years ago). Is it better to stick with the topic and within the section change time references, or is it better to ask all your "now" questions and then do the "5 years ago" questions? There is no one definitive answer to quandaries like this. In part you have to see what seems to make the most sense given your sequence of questions. In part, you have to try them out in a pretest and see which works best.

Within each major section you want to order the questions in some manner that has a logical sense to it. For instance, in the health insurance section you first want to ask whether respondents have health insurance, then which type of insurance they have, and then whether they share the costs with their employer, and finally how much they have to pay each month for health insurance. Play a game and think of other orders for these four questions. None of the alternative orders make as much sense, yet it is common to see questionnaires in which the sequence of questions would read much better after some judicious reordering.

The "flow" of the questions is also important to consider from the perspective of difficulty or sensitivity. Do not hit the respondent with very difficult or sensitive questions right off the bat. You have not established much trust yet; the respondent is still getting the hang of answering your questions. Start the questionnaire with some easy questions, ones that establish a context for the rest of the questionnaire. Another temptation is to leave the hard questions or the sensitive questions to the very end, in a sort of "hit and run" mentality. I do not recommend this primarily because I do not want respondents to be fatigued when they get to these important questions.

The best solution is to put them somewhere in the middle. In our AIDS risk assessment surveys we started by asking respondents who they had had discussions with about AIDS, and then we moved into some attitudinal questions before getting at knowledge questions. We moved into questions about their own sexual behavior (the most sensitive) and then wound down with some attitudinal questions about testing, finishing with some demographic items.

*   *   *

By following the guidelines described in this chapter and the previous one, you should produce a questionnaire that is easy to administer and that produces high quality data. Before we can collect the data, we need to have a sample of respondents. In the next two chapters we turn to sampling procedures.

4

The Basics of Sampling

There are two distinct groups in the survey sampling world—those who are strict adherents to random sampling methods and those who are not. The major advantages of random sampling methods are that you have a statistical basis for making statements about the population and you can easily calculate the limits of your confidence in these findings, based on the size of your sample. The major drawback is that to draw the samples correctly requires appropriate knowledge and skills as well as resources. The major advantage of nonrandom sampling methods is that they are easier to carry out and therefore significantly less expensive. Their major disadvantage is that you have no basis for knowing how well your sampled group represents the more general population that you are actually interested in.

The two most common forms of nonrandom sampling are convenience samples and quota samples. Each unfortunately has its attractions. Convenience samples are selected in a manner as their name implies—conveniently. You identify a group of people who are easy to gain access to. Unfortunately, in many instances, the group that is easily accessible is not necessarily the group that represents the population you are actually interested in. For instance, a "person on the street" sample is a convenience sample but it is not likely to be representative of the community. Other examples are giving surveys to students in your dorm or in your psychology class; again these groups are unlikely to be representative of college-aged youth or of college students in general. Supermarket surveys are convenience samples—surveying whoever happens to come to the store that day. This group is unlikely to be representative of shoppers or of the community. Convenience samples all have the same basic flaw: They are a very narrow subset of the population you are really interested in, and there is grave doubt about how representative they are of the total population.

The assumption that a "convenient" group is "good enough" to represent the population you want to talk about is really at the heart of the problem. It is a critical part of quality sampling to adequately define your population and then to carefully identify sources of lists that actually correspond to the population of interest. Users of convenience samples do not usually identify the limits of their findings in relation to their choice of sample population.

Another problem with convenience samples is that the interviewer, or person handing out the forms, has a lot of discretion over whom they approach. Without strict rules, surveyors tend to approach people who are like themselves and avoid those who are not.

Quota samples bend the rules of random sampling just "somewhat" and as such they may seem not quite so bad. In quota samples you usually impose a few goals for the characteristics of your sample, for example, targeting equal numbers of males and females and requiring about one in five be an elderly person. This ensures that on a few dimensions your sample "looks" like the population it is supposed to represent. The problem is that you can only establish "quotas" on a few dimensions, and even in doing so you have no guarantee that your sample represents the population on any other dimension. Also, just because your sample has 50% men and 50% women does not mean that the male respondents are a representative sample of all men or that the women are a representative sample of women. In a way the quotas make you think that you have imposed a measure of representativeness on your sample when in fact you have not really achieved much more than the convenience sample. Your data collectors are still free to pick the people who look like themselves.

The critical benefit of random sampling is that all types of people have a chance to be in your sample. You do not really have to work very hard to get this mix. By following random sampling procedures, the representative mix of your sample is an automatic outgrowth of the process.

To achieve random sampling you need to understand a few basic principles and to know how to carry out those principles in a pragmatic fashion. The following concepts are useful beginning points.

1. A random sample is unbiased in the sense that it gives everyone in the population a chance of falling into your sample.
2. Your sample can only be as good as the original list from which it was drawn. If your list is flawed, the sampling technique cannot overcome the flaw.
3. A random sample can vary in its representativeness, even though it is perfectly unbiased, just because of chance variations. How

likely your sample is to deviate from true representativeness is directly related to the absolute size of your sample.

SAMPLING FRAMES

The list that you draw your sample from is called a sampling frame. The goal is that everyone in the population that you are interested in studying is included on the list. The overall quality of your sample is limited by the quality of your list. The key issues that you worry about with your list are (a) is my list complete? and (b) even if my list is complete, does it encompass the population that I really want to make statements about?

Lists can be incomplete in a variety of ways. Ask yourself (and the maintainer of the list) who is left off the list entirely. Lists of students often leave off special students, graduate students, or part-time students. Do you want these kinds of students in your study? If so, you have a problem if the list leaves them out. Another example is trying to draw a sample using the phone book. People without phones are not listed, nor are people who pay extra to have an "unlisted" number. Most studies would be seriously flawed if you left out all the people who do not have phones and all the people who have unlisted numbers.

Sometimes lists are inadequate because they are out of date. Ask how often the list is updated and the process that has to be followed for someone to be added to the list. If it has been a while since the list has been updated, then you can be sure that there is a group of folks that you would like to have represented in your study but who will not be. If people have to take the initiative to get themselves on the list (like a registered voter list) or to update the information on the list (like telling the registrar or a draft board about a change of address), you can bet that there are serious problems with how up to date the list is.

What do you do if you have a bad list? First, you see if there is some way to supplement the list with another list of the people who are left out. For instance, the registrar also has lists of part-time students, special students, and graduate students. City halls maintain lists of "new construction" that list all the new apartments and houses that have been built that year. By doing a little digging and checking, often you can patch the holes in your list so that it makes sense to use it.

Second, you look for a new list that is better than the old list. Instead of a list of registered voters to represent the city's population, you might instead use the list of addresses from the city tax assessor's office. Third, in the worst of cases, you carry out the study with the list you have, but you redefine the population that you are trying to represent. You describe your study as reflecting people who have telephones and who list their telephones in the phone book as of October 1 of the last year rather than as reflecting all city residents.

SAMPLING ERROR

When you take a sample from a population as opposed to collecting information from everybody, there is a probability that your sample will not perfectly mirror the characteristics of the population just because of chance error. For instance, if your population is split exactly among males and females, even though you draw a random sample, you might wind up with a sample that is 52% males and 48% females. If you have used random sampling procedures, you can calculate the likelihood of that error and its effects.

The formula is fairly straightforward: The size of the error in estimating any particular characteristic of the population from your sample is dependent on two factors—how much variability, or variance, there is in the population on the particular characteristic and how large your sample is. The formula for the size of sampling error is:

$$\text{sampling error} = \sqrt{\frac{\text{variance}}{\text{size of sample}}}$$

It turns out that we can be 95% certain that the proportion of any characteristic in the actual population is within the range of the estimate that comes from our sample plus or minus two times the size of the sampling error. This is called a confidence interval, and it can be applied to all estimates from the survey as an indication of the precision of our study.

What is particularly noteworthy about this formula is how changes in variability and size of the sample change the amount of error. If we consider the variability of a population characteristic that has only two states (a binomial), such as gender (male or female) or age (below 30 or above 30), it turns out that the measure of variability is greatest when the binomial is distributed equally across categories and decreases as the distribution gets more skewed toward one end or the other (e.g., 10-90% or 90-10%). Therefore, looking at our sampling error formula, sampling error is greatest when both parts of the binomial are common, and it is the least when one part is rare and the other part very common. The size of the sample works in an interesting fashion to affect sampling error. Because the size of the sample is in the denominator of the formula, a bigger sample size means less error and a smaller sample size means bigger error. This makes sense. What is notable, however, is that because everything is under a square root sign, to reduce the amount of error by half, you have to *quadruple* the sample size. This leads to a curve that has a "diminishing return" shape. For instance, if you did not like the amount of error a sample size of 100 was going to give you, you could cut the error in half by using a sample of 400 instead. If you still were not happy with the amount of error, then you could cut it in half again by using a sample size of 1600. If you still were not happy, you would have to go to a sample size of 6400 to cut it in half again. At some point the marginal costs of cutting error in half go beyond the needs or resources of the study, and the researcher settles for that degree of precision that can be obtained within the reality of budgetary limitations.

One other thing is notable about the formula: There is nothing in it that relates to the proportion that your sample is of the whole population. That is because the math assumes you are drawing from an infinite population. For most cases, your population size is relatively large in relation to the sample size, so that this assumption is relatively accurate. In these cases the absolute sample size is the key, not how big a proportion the sample is of the whole.

If in special circumstances you are drawing a relatively large proportion of the whole (e.g., sampling half the students in your school), there is an adjustment factor that can be added to the formula and that reduces the estimate of error.

TYPES OF RANDOM SAMPLES

There are several different methods of drawing random samples: the basic method of "simple random sampling" method and several other strategies. Each of the other strategies we will talk about tries to "improve" the sampling process particularly as it relates to representativeness, while at the same time maintaining random sampling procedures.

Simple Random Sampling

A simple random sampling method is equivalent to putting numbered beans in a jar, shaking them up really well, and then reaching in blindfolded to pick out the "winners." In drawing a simple random sample everybody in the population is put in the "jar" and we draw out of that jar the sample that we need.

The way we actually draw the sample is to use a table of random numbers. These tables can be found in the back of most statistics books. Many computers also have random number series built into them. The following steps are used to draw your sample.

1. Figure out how many people you want in your sample (see the section later in this chapter about deciding sample sizes).
2. Get a list that has everyone on it who is a member of the population that you want to study.
3. Number the list from number "1" to the "last person." The last person's number determines how many digits wide your numbers are going to be when you read from the random number table (e.g., 2-digit numbers, 3-digit numbers, 4-digit numbers, etc.).
4. Randomly pick a place to start reading random numbers from your table. (Closing your eyes and stabbing the page with your pencil is one good way to do this.) Also, because the random numbers in a random number table can be read in any direction (up or down, right or left), you need to figure out which direction you are going to move in the table once you pick your starting point.
5. If you pick number "036," then the person whose number is "36" on your list is in your sample. Move to the next random number in the direction you predetermined to get your next random number. If your next pick is number "413" then the person whose number is "413" is also in your sample.
6. Keep picking (moving back and forth between the table of random numbers and your numbered list) until you get the sample size that you want.

There are two issues that researchers worry about when they think about using simple random sampling methods—the amount of drudgery work involved in numbering lists and looking up lots of numbers in a random number table; and the representativeness of the sample. Drudgery can be solved by computerizing the process.

Representativeness is limited by the two factors we discussed earlier—the amount of variability and the size of your sample. When we select our random sample, whatever we measure about this sample in our study will have a confidence interval around our estimates of plus or minus two standard errors. As long as we use simple random sampling procedures, there will always be this limit on the precision of our sample estimates. There are other random sampling methods that do a better job of guaranteeing representativeness, because they limit the amount of sampling error. We will discuss these next.

Systematic Random Sampling

A systematic random sample addresses both concerns raised above: It involves less drudgery to draw the sample and often the resulting sample is more representative of the population. Let me first explain how this sampling method is easier to produce. The steps are as follows.

1. Obtain a list of the population that you want to study.
2. Number the list. (In fact, this step is not absolutely necessary but it makes things a little easier if each member of the population is numbered.)
3. Decide how big you want your sample to be.
4. Figure out the fraction that your sample is of the whole population. For instance, you may want to draw a sample of 1000 households from the list you have obtained from city hall, 20,000 households in all. Therefore your sample is 1/20th of the total. The key to the technique is how you read this fraction: Instead of 1/20th, read it as 1 out of 20. Twenty is the "interval." What you want to do is to think of your entire list as the sum of many smaller sublists that are each 20 units in size. What you want to do is to take 1 randomly selected household from each of the sublists of 20 units.
5. Go to your random number table and randomly select one number within the interval (in this case a number between 1 and 20). Let us imagine that you did that and you chose number "7." This is called your random start.
6. The first household in your sample is the seventh household listed in the first sublist of 20 units.

7. Now this next step is the secret of systematic sampling. You continue down your list, taking the 7th-listed household in each of your sublists of 20 units. You first took the 7th household (the 7th household in the first group of 20 units). Then you take as your next household the 27th household on the list (the 7th household in the next group of 20 units), then the 47th (the 7th household in the third group of 20 units), and so on until you get to the end of the list.

You will have taken 1 out of 20 all the way down the list, and your sample will therefore be 1/20th of the whole. As you may have noticed if you were following the steps closely, we entered the random number table only once to get our random start; this is clearly easier than going into the random table a thousand times.

The other outcome of this process that is important is the pattern of our selections. Because we took 1 out of 20 all the way down the list, our selections are very evenly spaced throughout the list. We have just as many selections in the first quarter of the list as we do in the last quarter of the list. If you will, we have sampled all parts of the list equally and with certainty. No part of the list was left unsampled, nor did any part of the list get "oversampled." It is this feature that potentially improves the representativeness of the sample.

The key to whether we can improve the representativeness of the sample, in comparison to simple random sampling methods, is whether the list that we sampled from has an *order* to it. Sometimes the lists have obvious orderings (e.g., lists that are alphabetized), and sometimes the lists have an order that is more subtle, so you have to track down how the list was constructed (e.g., a list of patients in a hospital may be ordered by the day that they were admitted, or a list of employees may be ordered by ZIP code or home address). Whatever mechanism is used to order the list, our systematic sample will have zero sampling error on that characteristic. The reason for this comes back to the pattern of evenly spaced selections throughout the list. There is no way that by chance we could get too many picks from one part of the list or too few from another part. Therefore, the sample is perfectly representative of the characteristic that orders the list.

The benefits of reduced sampling error can extend beyond the characteristic that defines the ordering of the list. Any other characteristic that is related to the one that orders the list also benefits from a reduction of sampling error. How much of a reduction is made will depend on how strong the second characteristic relates to the one that orders the list. Usually it turns out that there are lots of characteristics that are related.

For instance, if you have a list that is alphabetized by last name, then you will reduce your sampling error on ethnic background (all those Irish names grouped together—O'Neil, O'Henry, McNeil, McHenry, etc.), and therefore indirectly on religious background, and in turn on any other characteristic that is correlated with these factors, such as values, dietary habits, eye color, and so on.

Another example would be a list that comes from the registrar of a college where students are listed by year in school. This would also produce a sample with less sampling error on such factors as age, experience with the school, maturity, job experience, and acquired academic knowledge.

There is only one caution concerning systematic random sampling. A serious problem will arise in drawing your sample if for some reason your list is ordered with some kind of repeating, cyclical order *and* your sampling interval overlaps that cycle. An example will demonstrate this problem. Let us say that you have a list of married people from which you want to draw a sample. If the list is ordered wife (1), husband (1), wife (2), husband (2), and so on, *and* if your sampling interval is an *even* number (1 out of 20, 1 out of 100, or 1 out of 500, for example), then you will wind up with a sample of all wives or all husbands depending on your random start number. Clearly a sample of married people is not representative if you include only wives or only husbands.

The way to avoid this issue is first to inspect your list and think about how it is ordered. If there is any cycle to the ordering, figure out what its frequency is. When you select your sampling interval, check to make sure that the cycle frequency is not some multiple of the sampling interval that you need to use. If there is not any overlap, then there is no issue with using systematic methods to draw your sample. If there is an overlap, then something needs to be changed, either the sampling interval you choose or the ordering of your list (but not by too much because this will destroy the positive effects that derive from the order).

Holding aside the one problem that might occur with cyclical order-ings, systematic random sampling holds open the possibility of improv-ing the quality of your sample just by knowing when to take advantage of the fact that a list might have an order to it. Of course, not all lists have an order, or the factor that it is ordered on may have little interest for your topic of study. In this case, systematic random sampling will not produce better representativeness than a simple random sample (it will not be any worse either, however), but it still will be easier to draw the sample if you are doing so by hand.

Stratified Random Sampling

This method of sampling is the strongest tool we have to reduce sampling error. It takes the underlying concept about ordering of the list (or putting people together in similar groupings) that we discussed above and carries it further than what we can do with systematic random sampling. What you need to do to achieve the benefits of stratified random sampling is to purposely *reorder* your list such that you create subgroups (or strata) in which people are identical on some characteristic. By creating these subgroups, you provide the possibility of sampling each of these subgroups in exactly the proportion that they are in the population as a whole. Therefore your sample is perfectly representative of these grouping characteristics and has no sampling error on these dimensions.

In addition, every characteristic that is related to your stratification characteristic also is incorporated in your sample with reduced sampling error. How much of a reduction in sampling error is realized depends on how strongly the characteristic is related to the stratification characteristic.

It is possible to use several characteristics simultaneously to stratify your sample. For instance, you might get a list from the registrar at a college that first divides the students into freshmen, sophomores, juniors, and seniors, then subdivides each of these groups into male and female subgroups, and then in turn divides them into groups based on the type of campus housing they have (dorm, townhouse, off-campus apartment, etc.).

Stratification is always a good thing to do. It always reduces sampling error. What is the catch then? Why isn't this the only sampling method that people use? The problem is that in order to stratify the list, the information about strata membership has to be included as part of the original list so that the list can be reorganized along the dimensions you want. Many times you get access to lists that do not have additional information from which to stratify, or the information that is available does not seem to be at all relevant to your study issues.

To summarize the technique:

1. Obtain a list of the population that you want to sample that also includes stratification information.

2. Sort, or reorder, the list so that you create separate groups defined by values of the stratification variable.
3. Number your list. (You can number your list in two different ways: (a) You can number consecutively through the whole population moving from one group to the next or (b) you can number each strata from 1 to "*n*." If you do it this last way you then have a choice of techniques for the next step.)
4. If you have numbered your list consecutively you then go on to draw your sample by using the systematic random sampling procedures. Figure out how many you want in each group and calculate a sampling interval, then pick a random start from a table of random numbers and apply the interval throughout the list. If you have numbered your list only within each separate strata you can do a series of systematic samples within each group, or you can draw a simple random sample within each stratum, selecting the exact number that you need from each stratum to perfectly represent the proportion of that group to the whole.

Unequal Rates of Selection

In the discussion above we described procedures that used the same sampling fraction within each stratum. For most samples this is the goal. There are some occasions, however, when there are advantages to sampling at different rates within strata. Sometimes there is a stratum that makes up a relatively small proportion of the whole population but for which there are important analyses to be conducted. Particularly if these analyses call for further subdividing that group, you may want more cases from that stratum than you would get from applying the overall sampling rate.

Because each of the strata is identified, it is easy to apply a larger sampling rate to this small subgroup. Instead of 1 out of 10 you might use a rate of 1 out of 3 or even take 100% of them. This oversampling would provide more cases for your analysis from this stratum.

There are two "problems" with this technique. First, when you present answers for the sample as a whole you have to adjust for the fact that you have selected too many cases from a particular stratum. You need to restore that group to its proper size in relation to the other strata. This is a relatively easy procedure to carry out from within many common statistical computer programs. The process is called weighting, and it statistically downsizes your oversampled group so that its proper proportion to the sample as a whole is restored.

An example of this might be helpful. Let us say that in your sample of college students you realized that "part-time" students represented only 5% of the population. You might oversample them so that they actually represent 20% of your sample. When you want to report information about the whole population of students you have to adjust the weight of the part-time students because they are contributing too much to the answers as a result of the oversampling. You want to weight each of their answers by 1/4 so that they are restored to the proper proportion of the total student body.

The second problem relates to the "real" size of your sample. The sampling error calculation assumes a simple random sample—all parts to the population have an equal probability of selection. By weighting your oversampled group down to the size that it should have been, you effectively reduce your overall sample size, and this increases your sampling error. For instance, if you sampled a group at a rate of 1 in 5 and wound up with 100 cases when they "should" have been sampled at a rate of 1 in 20 with 25 cases selected, by weighting you will reduce your overall sample size by 75 cases. Because many statistical calculations are based on the sample size, oversampling has a cost in that it reduces the effective sample size of your overall sample.

Multistage Sampling

This next method of sampling does not produce a "better" sample than any of the methods described above; however, it does produce a better sample than what the *practical* alternatives would give. Each of the alternative sampling methods described above started with the same instruction: Obtain a list of the entire population and number it. Many times this first step is an onerous one, or even an impossible one, because of the size of the population. All households in the United States or all college students or all patients in hospitals suggest only a few examples of lists that are impossible or impractical to obtain.

Given this practical impediment, many researchers give up on true random sampling and start using the nonrandom sampling methods that we mentioned at the beginning of the chapter. The question becomes, how do you manage to draw a random sample when it is impossible to get a complete list, or at least impractical to consider obtaining the whole list of the population? It is the solution to this problem that multistage sampling provides, thereby creating a "better" sample than what the alternatives would produce.

The secret to multistage sampling is, as the name implies, to draw your sample in stages. What is necessary, because at the outset it is impractical to get a list of the whole population, is to aggregate the population into clumps or groups of which you can get a list and to sample these groups first and then try to get the lists for the groups that you have picked.

For example, let us say that you wanted to draw a national sample of college students. There is no preexisting list of all college students, so it is impossible to immediately draw the sample. It *is* possible to get a list of all colleges. The first step then is to get that list, number the list of colleges, and randomly select some of those colleges (using any of the random sampling methods you have learned about). Now that you have a smaller list of colleges, you would contact each of them, get a list of their students, and select a random sample of the students from each college that you had sampled.

It is possible to add additional stages to the process to make the process as feasible as possible. In the example above, for instance, you could have first sampled states, then sampled colleges within each selected state, then sampled students within each of the selected colleges.

The key component of these procedures is that the higher aggregating units (e.g., states or colleges) must span the entire population that you are ultimately interested in sampling (e.g., college students). The procedure then is just a repetition of the same steps—get a list, number it, and select a sample, then repeat the steps for the next stage.

One of the usual goals of a random sampling method is that every unit in the population has an equal chance of selection. In order to calculate the overall probability of selection for an individual, one must multiply the probabilities of selection at each stage in the process. To achieve the goal of equal chances of selection when using multistage sampling methods, the following possible procedures can be used.

Method A

In any of the stages before the last stage, units are selected without regard to size (e.g., states or colleges). In the last stage, however, you want to select the same *proportion* of students from each college. For example, the probability of selection in our study of college students might be:

$$\frac{1}{5} \text{ states} \times \frac{1}{30} \text{ colleges} \times 1\% \text{ students} = \frac{1}{15,000} \text{ students}$$

A careful student of sampling will realize that in the first couple of stages of this method, college students in large states or large colleges do not have any greater chance of falling into the sample than students in small states or small colleges, although as a group they make up a large number of students. This problem is compensated for in the last stage by taking more students from larger schools than from smaller schools. The net result is that students, no matter what size state or college they attend, have the same probability of falling into our sample.

Method B—Multistage Sampling Proportionate to Size

In this method we consider the size of the aggregating unit as part of each preliminary stage to give schools with large numbers of students a higher chance of being selected in the first stages than schools with smaller numbers of students. In order to use this method the list of aggregating units must also contain the number of the final sampling units that are contained within the aggregating unit. For instance, we would need to know how many college students attend schools within each of the 50 states, as well as to know how many students attend the various colleges within the states selected in the first stage.

In order to achieve an equal probability of selection after all stages are completed, the sampling procedure requires selecting an *equal number* of students from each college in the *last* stage of the sampling process. If our sampling strategy wound up picking 20 colleges nationwide, then we might choose 100 students from each of these colleges to be in our study. By following these procedures one of the magic elements is realized—the size of the aggregating unit ultimately makes no impact on the probability of being in our final sample. The following formula may help you see why this is:

$$
\underset{\text{1st Stage}}{\underbrace{\frac{\text{\# States}}{\text{Selected}} \times \frac{\text{Size of State}}{\text{Size of Population}}}} \times \underset{\text{2nd Stage}}{\underbrace{\frac{\text{\# Colleges}}{\text{Selected}} \times \frac{\text{Size of College}}{\text{Size of State}}}} \times \underset{\text{3rd Stage}}{\underbrace{\frac{\text{\# Students Picked}}{\text{Size of College}}}}
$$

You can see in this formula that the two aggregating unit sizes (size of state and size of college) cancel in the formula so that the final probability of selection for every student is:

$$
\frac{\text{\# States Selected} \times \text{\# Colleges Selected} \times \text{\# Students Picked at Each}}{\text{Size of Population}}
$$

HOW BIG SHOULD YOUR SAMPLE BE?

Anybody who plans a survey project has to deal with this question eventually. For many research projects, the sample size is decided by how much the budget can afford. This may not be the best way to decide how big your sample should be. Instead, there are statistically based strategies that will guide you in making this decision.

Before we explain these statistical strategies, it is useful to warn you that these are guidelines and must be looked at in the context of the whole project. There are several problems with these approaches. First, they give the appearance of irrefutable science when in fact they are merely guidelines. Second, they give an answer that addresses minimum sample sizes, not necessarily optimum sizes. Third, they assume that a study is being done to look at one variable, when in fact many variables might be equally important. Fourth, they imply that the only error in a study comes from sampling error and therefore give a false sense of precision. Keeping these problems in mind will help you use the statistical guidelines for their intended purpose.

The mathematical formulas for choosing sample sizes are very closely tied to the sampling error formula we presented on page 41. Remember that there were two factors that affected sampling error—the amount of variability of a characteristic in the population and the size of the sample. One approach to selecting sample size is to use this formula but to solve for size of sample. You have to estimate the variance that you expect (or use a worst case scenario by assuming a binomial variable with a 50%-50% distribution), and you have to select the precision that you want in your survey estimates. By using this formula we find the size of the sample needed to produce a given level of sampling error under our variance assumptions. Remember that if you want greater precision, sample size must increase; for example, a sampling error reduced by half means that the sample size goes up by a factor of four.

The other statistical approach is called a power calculation, and it is done in the context of how you are going to use your data. If you are doing your survey because you want to compare two groups and decide if they are "different" on some characteristic, then one of your concerns is how confident can you be in your findings. In particular, the power calculations tell us how certain we can be that a *no difference* finding is real. It turns out that you cannot both maximize power and the ability to detect a significant difference; basically, for a given sample size, the higher one is the lower the other is (Cohen, 1988, p. 4).

Both statistical strategies, though, need to be tempered with our knowledge about the weaknesses of these strategies. We have to remember that we have many variables in our studies, not just one; we have to remember that there are more sources of error than sampling error and therefore that some of our resources should be devoted to reducing those types of error. Finally, we should remember that many of our analyses are not done on the whole sample but instead focus on comparisons of subgroups. If these analyses are in fact the key analyses to be done, then the sample size calculations should address how big these subgroups will wind up being and consider whether this size is sufficient to sustain the analyses that you want to do.

5

Pitfalls in Sampling

In this chapter we discuss some problems that you may run into when selecting your sample, so that you can be prepared to resolve them. We have alluded to some of these issues in the earlier chapters, but we want to emphasize them here.

OUT-OF-DATE LISTS

Out-of-date lists can cause efficiency problems for your study and can also seriously damage the quality of your study. One way in which lists are out of date is that there are "extra" people on the list. People who have left the organization or who no longer live in the city, for example, or people who have died may still be listed, but the likelihood of any of these persons responding to your survey is low. In addition, you may not get information sent back (from the post office or a relative or the person themselves) that lets you know that they received a survey and they should not have. Therefore, you waste resources by sending reminders (not to mention the original package) to people who should not be getting the surveys.

In addition, however, the quality of your study may be affected. Your calculation of overall response rates will be artificially low, because there are people in the denominator who should not be.

The primary strategy for dealing with this problem is awareness. You need to talk with the person who is responsible for the list about the updating process. How often is the list updated, and whose initiative is it to remove persons from the list? You also want to know the consequences of the list being out of date to the organization that keeps the list. These questions will help you zero in on likely problems and give you an idea of how extensive these problems might be.

Another strategy that is useful is to pilot your study to check out the quality of the list. If you put on your envelope "do not forward—return to sender" or "address correction requested," you will find out how many people are not at the addresses listed very quickly. You may also want to include with the pilot survey a postcard that says "I cannot participate in your survey because . . . " This will provide you with feedback on the problems that people have with doing the study, among which may be responses that say people are not currently part of the population.

Another way that lists can be out of date is that they do not have recent additions to the population included in the list. Someone who has recently moved into the community or someone who has just been hired by a company may not yet be on the list. Again, the primary way of discovering this problem is to talk with the person responsible for putting together the list. Ask about the cycle of updating: How often does that happen? Sometimes the lists are updated continuously but there is a lag time between the event and the revision of the list. One example that I am keenly aware of is the department of vital records and how quickly lists are updated about births. Parents fill out the birth certificate information at the hospital, the hospital sends the form to the department of vital records, this form gets keypunched, and then the record gets added to the computer system. Given how many steps along the way there are, and the inevitable problems, it is not surprising to know that a child may not be added to the lists of births until about three months after that child is born.

Remember that the quality of your data is affected because you are leaving a segment of the population out of your study; often these people may be among the most critical for your study to include. For example, our birth certificate example above probably has a longer lag time for families that have home births.

Once you identify the method by which the list is updated and the potential problems, issues, and delays, you can map out a strategy to overcome these problems. One solution is to consider getting a complete list or a list that is somehow more likely to be accurate. I was involved in a study of a corporation in which the list of employees that we obtained from the personnel office was said to be "very up to date." As we began our study and learned about the number of dead people, retired people, and people on extended leave that were still on our list, we asked some hard questions of the company that we should have asked in the first place. What we discovered was that the company had *two* lists—the list that we had gotten from personnel and the list maintained by the payroll office. We found out that most of the efforts by the company to keep its list updated were devoted to the payroll list. We would have been better off to use that list instead of the one we used. In this study we also needed information that was only on the personnel list (which was the reason we were pointed toward that list in the first place). Ideally we would have obtained both lists and moved the information we needed from the personnel list to the payroll list, which had a more up-to-date listing of active employees and their current work locations. The notion that there may be more than one list available is not an unusual one. Cities have a variety of lists of their residents—voter registration, tax rolls, public works, school department—and then there are lists of residents other than those compiled by the cities, such as commercial directories (for use by insurance salespersons and real estate agents) and lists compiled by the telephone company, other utility companies, the registry of motor vehicles, and other groups. Your job is to identify the possible sources of the lists, investigate the quality of the alternatives, and choose the one list or combination of lists that will produce the most up-to-date list for use in selecting your sample.

BIASES RESULTING
FROM LACK OF COVERAGE

Leaving people out of your list of the population (and therefore leaving them out of your sample) is called a coverage problem. Your study sample does not match the population that you think it does. Usually, this problem creates a bias in your data. Sometimes the bias is small or not a particular problem for your study. For instance, using a department of motor vehicles' list to do a study of drunk driving attitudes leaves out people who have not applied for a driver's license (assuming we have the suspended license subgroup in the list). The study therefore leaves out nondrivers. That may not be that bad, particularly if the focus is on the views of drivers. Of course, we are still leaving out the people who drive but have never applied for their license, but this may not be a big issue.

We are also leaving out all the drivers who have out-of-state licenses. In a college town this may be a large number of drivers and drivers that you are particularly interested in including in your study. When the group left out is large, then the potential bias in your data is also large.

Let us discuss another example of a faulty list that creates a problem. What if you wanted to study teenage drug use? Obtaining a list of students from the school department may at first seem like a good idea. The problem, however, is the dropouts. Clearly this is an important subgroup whose behavior would be important to include in your study of teenage drug habits. It may be that the school department has records of students who should be in school but who have dropped out so that your list can be supplemented. The key is that you have to realize whom you have left out and then begin figuring out how to incorporate those types in your sample.

To emphasize this point, the people that are most likely to be left off the list are probably different from the people on the list on one or another characteristic. You have to evaluate how different you think these people are and how leaving them out might affect the usefulness of your study. It may be that leaving them out is a critical flaw. If so, you have to look for a way to get a better list. On the other hand, leaving them out may not be that much of a problem. Your responsibility, however, is to describe accurately the population that you are studying. For our sample of licensed drivers above, we would say that our study is a study of persons who have driver's licenses in the state, not that our study is a study of the residents of that state.

SAMPLING SPECIFIC PEOPLE
VERSUS SPECIFIC ADDRESSES

If your sampling frame is a list of persons who work for a company, or who were patients at a health center, or who were students at a school, as examples, then clearly you are sampling people and you address the envelope to a specific individual. For the most part you assume that if you get the questionnaire back, it was indeed filled out by the person to whom you addressed it.

If your sample is a sample of households, then we have a different issue. First you have to decide if your intention is to do a study of "people" or of "households." Now of course a person is still filling out the questionnaire, even though it is about the "household," but the issue is that in a household survey we do not care which household member fills out the survey. In a people survey we want to have a specific person fill out the survey in each household.

There are two ways to achieve this goal. One strategy is to designate the type of person—the oldest male, the husband, the wife, the head of the household, the youngest adult, the person who uses the local recreational facilities the most, and so on. There are two potential problems with this type of strategy: (a) you depend on people in the household to follow your instructions and (b) you need to have a plan "B" set of instructions when there is not someone like that living in the household.

The other strategy is to select randomly one adult from the household. The easiest way to do this is to use a random indicator and ask household members to implement it. One of the easiest mechanisms to use is "the adult in the household whose birthday is closest to today's date." Of course, you still have to depend on the people in the household following your instructions.

WEIGHTING RESPONSES

There are two sampling decisions that you might make that will require you to weight your data. Weighting your data means that you count some responses more heavily than others. We need to do this when our sampling design gives some people a greater chance of being in our sample than other people; by weighting we restore everybody to an "equal probability" status.

The first example of a sampling decision that would require weighting is a stratified random sample in which you have used different rates of selection across strata. Suppose in a study of college students we had selected 20% of freshmen and sophomores but 30% of juniors and seniors. This would result in a sample that had more juniors and seniors in it than we were supposed to. (We might make such a decision because some of our analyses might be done only on juniors and seniors and this way we would ensure getting enough of them to support our analytic goals.) If we do analyses that attempt to describe the sample as a whole (e.g., the campuswide answer to question #10 is . . .), then it would be incorrect to present information that is too heavily weighted toward the answers given by juniors and seniors.

To correct this "problem," we need to either increase the apparent numbers of freshmen and sophomores or decrease the apparent numbers of juniors and seniors, or do a combination of both. The easiest approach is to increase one group or to decrease the other one; the most statistically correct solution is to alter both groups. If we wanted to increase the weight for freshmen and sophomores to be equivalent to that of juniors and seniors, then we have to "weight" their answers by 1.5 (30% divided by 20% sampling rates). In essence what we instruct the computer to do is to "count" each freshman and sophomore's answers 1.5 times. Computer programs often used by social scientists, such as SAS and SPSS, make it easy to carry out this procedure. If we wanted to adjust both groups, then the freshmen and sophomores would need to have their weight *increased* by a factor of 1.25 (25% average rate of selection divided by the 20% actual rate of selection) and the juniors and seniors would need to have their weight *decreased* by a factor of .83 (25% average rate of selection divided by the 30% actual rate of selection).

The second example of a sampling decision that requires weighting is a design in which you want to study a population of people but you randomly selected households from a list and then within the household you asked one person to fill out the questionnaire. In this situation, people in differently sized households have different probabilities of being included in your sample. Respondents in two-person households have 1 chance in 2 of being in (after you have selected their household), whereas respondents in four-person households have only 1 chance in 4 of being in the study. The easiest way to compensate is to weight the answers by the number of eligible respondents within each household; this means weighting the answers by "2" in a two-person household and by "4" in a four-person household. The more statistically correct "weights" to use would be to adjust each weight by dividing by the average weight for the whole sample.

Anytime you intend to *describe* your population by presenting statistics such as means or percentages or rates, then it is critical that you employ weighting procedures if you used unequal probabilities of selection. Otherwise, you will not be describing your population accurately. On the other hand, analyses such as correlations or regressions do not usually require you to weight your data because you are testing whether a relationship exists and not trying to describe the population. Analyses searching for relationships usually are not thrown off by unequal probabilities of selection and therefore do not usually need to be weighted.

6

The Basics of Avoiding Nonresponse Errors

NONRESPONSE ERROR

Just because you draw a large, random sample does not mean that your data are perfectly valid. Another potential source of error beyond sampling error is nonresponse error. This error is caused by failing to get a return from 100% of your sample and the fact that there are differences between those who respond to your survey and those who do not. The size of this error is dependent, therefore, on how big the nonresponse is and how different the nonresponders are from the responders (Armstrong & Overton, 1977; Barnette, 1950; Baur, 1947; Bishop, Hippler, Schwartz, & Stack, 1988; Blair, 1964; Blumberg, Fuller, & Hare, 1974; Brennan & Hoek, 1992; Campbell, 1949; Champion & Sear, 1969; Clausen & Ford, 1947; Cox, Anderson, & Fulcher, 1974; Daniel, 1975; Dillman, 1978; Donald, 1960; Eichner & Habermehl, 1981; Filion, 1975; Gannon, Northern, & Carrol, 1971; Gough & Hall, 1977; Jones & Lang, 1980; Larson & Catton, 1959; Newman, 1962; Ognibene, 1970; Reuss, 1943; Suchman & McCandless, 1940).

Nonresponse error is the single biggest impediment to any survey study, but it is particularly a risk for mail surveys. Unfortunately, in many studies very little is known about the nonresponders and therefore we are left with uncertainty about the quality of the data. The solution to this concern is to do everything in your power to conduct a study that has a very high response rate. By obtaining a very high response rate, it is very unlikely that the nonresponders will have an impact on the validity of your population estimates even if the nonresponders were different.

What is considered a high response rate? Certainly a response rate in excess of 85% is viewed as an excellent rate of return. It would need a peculiar set of circumstances to throw off your results by very much. Response rates in the 70% to 85% range are viewed as very good. Responses in the 60% to 70% range are considered acceptable, but you begin to be uneasy about the characteristics of nonresponders. Response rates between 50% and 60% are barely acceptable and really need some additional information that contributes to confidence about the quality of your data. Response rates below 50% really are not scientifically acceptable. After all, a majority of the sample is not represented in your results.

Besides ensuring high response rates, it is always a useful effort to try to obtain information about the nonresponders so that you can compare them to responders. Sometimes this information is available from the list that you originally sampled. For instance, city lists that are used to confirm eligibility for voter registration have the person's age, gender (you can usually figure it out from first names), occupation in broad categories, precinct or voting district, whether the person is registered to vote or not, and, if registered, party affiliation. By keeping track of who has and has not responded from your original sample, you can compare the characteristics of those who did respond with those who did not respond.

Sometimes you can obtain small amounts of information from nonresponders as a supplement to the original data collection effort. You have to limit yourself to a few indicators, and you have to make it very easy for the person to respond. You may even need to include some type of incentive. In choosing which indicators to try to collect information about, you want to select questions that are easy to answer and make a big difference in your results. It is very important to include questions that describe the demographic characteristics of your sample *as well as* some key questions about the central issue you are studying. This allows you to compare directly nonresponders and responders on the key concepts as well as to compare indirectly on any question that is correlated with demographic characteristics. On a study of alcohol use, we asked nonresponders to tell us their age, gender, marital status, education, current frequency of drinking (in broad categories), and whether they had ever had a drinking problem. We sent the one-page questionnaire along with $2, and we received a 50% return from among those people who had not responded to our survey.

Based on our study and others (Baur, 1947; Campbell, 1949; Gannon et al., 1971; Gelb, 1975; Goodstadt, Chung, Kronitz, & Cook, 1977; Ognibene, 1970; Peterson, 1975; Robins, 1963; Suchman, 1962), we can get a picture of the usual type of nonresponder. They tend to be less educated, or elderly, or unmarried, or male, or to have some characteristic that makes them seem less relevant to the study (e.g., abstainers for a drinking study, nondrivers for a traffic safety study, or lower-income people on a study about mortgages).

The reason that these types tend to be nonresponders are common-sensical. The less educated may be intimidated by the survey process or have less appreciation for the value of research. The elderly may have trouble filling out the questionnaire, and on average they have less education than the rest of the population. They also may be more suspicious of the purposes of the research. Unmarrieds and males may feel like they have less time to fill out a questionnaire, and males perhaps are somewhat less cooperative as a group than are females. People who have characteristics that seem to make the study less relevant to them may feel that their participation is less important, or they may be less interested in the issues.

Nonresponse errors create problems for your study in two ways. First, if people who do not respond hold different views or behave differently from the majority of people, your study will incorrectly report the population average. It will also drastically underreport the number of people who feel as the nonresponders do. The basic problem is that nonresponders make your picture of the population wrong. How far off the mark you are depends on the pattern of nonresponse, but in any event your findings will not be accurate.

Even if nonresponders are not that different from responders, low response rates give the appearance of a poor quality study and shake the consumer's confidence in the results of the study. The study becomes less useful or less influential because it does not have the trappings of quality.

As we said above, nonresponse error is a major problem with mail surveys. The major reason that mail surveys are vulnerable to nonresponse error is that it is *very* easy for a person not to respond to a mail survey. It is not like you have to close a door in someone's face, or even hang up the phone on a persistent interviewer; all you have to do is throw it in the waste basket. In addition, you can also become a nonresponder just because you never got around to filling out that questionnaire.

All levels of response rates are reported in the literature. It is safe to assume that some of the worst response rates never see the light of an academic journal. If the only thing you did was to put a questionnaire in an envelope and ask people to fill it out, it would be common to see response rates in the 20% range, and it would not be surprising to see them in the 5% range. This is a long way from the 75% or so response rates that inspire confidence in data. How do you get better response rates? Is it just luck, or is there some magic formula that produces success? It turns out that there are some very specific things that you can, and must, do to achieve good response rates.

HOW TO GET GOOD RESPONSE RATES

There are a variety of procedures that all mail surveys should use to ensure that they obtain good response rates. We will describe each of these in this chapter. In the following chapter, we will describe other mechanisms that you can use to increase your response rates even further.

A Good Respondent Letter

Because most mail surveys arrive in the mail without any prior contact, the respondent letter has to do all the work of explaining the study and the general procedures, as well as motivating the respondent to participate (Andreasen, 1970; Champion & Sear, 1969; Hornik, 1981; Houston & Nevin, 1977; Simon, 1967). It is critical that you produce a respondent letter that is "just right." There are several elements that need to be included in the letter, and there are several things that you want to make sure you say.

1. The letter should not be too long. Keep it to one page.
2. Use professionally produced letterhead that makes it clear who is sending out the survey and who the supporting institution is. Do not just refer to a study name (e.g., The Healthy Family Study). Instead, include the name of the university or research institution as well.
3. Make it clear how people can get in touch with you if they have questions. You need a name of a contact person. You need a phone number, perhaps even an "800" number or the instruction to "call collect."
4. You need to have a "grabber" as your first sentence, something that encourages the respondent to read the rest of the letter. In a study of police officers concerning gambling enforcement policies, we started with: "We'd like the benefit of your professional experience and ten minutes of your time!" For a corporate study of alcohol policies we started with: "Many people are concerned about alcohol abuse in the workplace."

5. You need to tell the respondent why this study is important and how this information may be used. Respondents want to participate only in things that they think are important and useful and that they feel relate to their lives in some specific way.
6. You need to explain who is being asked to participate in the survey and how you got their name and address.
7. You need to explain whether this is a confidential survey or an anonymous survey (they are not the same thing), and you need to explain how you are achieving confidentiality or anonymity.
8. You need to mention that participation in the study is voluntary, but also you should emphasize the importance of participation.
9. You need to make it clear how to get the questionnaire back to you.
10. You want to make sure that your letter is easy to read in terms of type size, layout, reproduction quality, and language level.

By following these suggestions for respondent letters, you should get your study off on the right foot.

Return Postage

It almost goes without saying that to get a good return rate you have to supply the respondent with a return envelope, already addressed to you, and return postage. (See Armstrong & Lusk, 1987; Brook, 1978; Gullahorn & Gullahorn, 1963; Harris & Guffey, 1978; Kernan, 1971; Kimball, 1961; McCrohan & Lowe, 1981; Peterson, 1975; Vocino, 1977; Yammarino, Skinner, & Childers, 1991.) You have two options for return postage. You can place a postage stamp on the return envelope or you can use a business reply envelope. Placing the postage stamp on the envelope puts subtle pressure on the respondent to send back the questionnaire so that the "stamp will not go to waste." The risk you run is that if they do not return the questionnaires, you have "wasted" the money on the unused stamps.

Business reply envelopes are efficient to use. You only get charged by the post office for the questionnaires that come back. You do have to set up an account with the post office first, and there are strict rules about how the envelope should be laid out, but business reply envelopes make the mailing process simple for the respondent.

In the next chapter we will discuss how different types of postage make an impact on your return rate.

Confidentiality/Anonymity

Respondents are generally more likely to respond if they feel that their answers are kept confidential instead of being attributed to them directly (Boek & Lade, 1963; Bradt, 1955; Childers & Skinner, 1985; Cox et al., 1974; Fuller, 1974; Futrell & Hise, 1982; Futrell & Swan, 1977; Kerin & Peterson, 1977; McDaniel & Jackson, 1981; Pearlin, 1961; Rosen, 1960; Wildman, 1977). There are some fairly direct methods for maintaining confidentiality. First, you do not put any names or addresses directly on the questionnaires themselves. Instead, put some kind of code number on the survey. The list of names and addresses with the corresponding code numbers can be kept separately and out of view of people who are not on the research team.

Second, when the questionnaires come back, do not leave them lying around for curious eyes to read. Instead, keep them in file cabinets, preferably locked when you are not around, and lock your office when you are not there.

Third, do not tell colleagues, friends, or family the answers from individual questionnaires.

Fourth, do not present data in reports or papers that allow readers to figure out who people are. Sometimes this means describing individuals with characteristics somewhat different from those they really have, or it sometimes means not presenting information on very small groups of people. For example, in a company report you would not present data on the group of three vice-presidents by saying "two thirds of the senior management group reported thinking about changing jobs in the next year." Data being presented for groups such as companies, schools, or hospitals should be presented without the groups being named unless there was a prior specific agreement that this would be done.

Maintaining anonymity is distinctly different from maintaining confidentiality. For confidentiality *you* know who filled out which questionnaire, but you promise not to divulge that information to anyone outside the research team. For anonymity, even you do not know which questionnaire belongs to which person. This is achieved by not putting any code number on the questionnaire before it is sent out. This way there is no link between the questionnaire and any sample list you have.

It seems logical that studies that could offer true anonymity (no identification numbers on the questionnaires) versus those that offer only confidentiality (a promise of no disclosure) would produce better response rates. Studies have not clearly proved such advantages (Andreasen,

1970; Boek & Lade, 1963; Bradt, 1955; Mason, Dressel, & Bain, 1961; Pearlin, 1961; Rosen, 1960; Scott, 1961). Perhaps this is too technical a distinction for respondents to understand. Perhaps they assume because you knew how to mail the questionnaire to them, you can somehow find them again if you want to. There is also the cynical interpretation that says "they could figure out who I am by putting together several demographic characteristics, so their promise of anonymity is really not much more than a promise of confidentiality." Finally, many surveys are rather innocuous, and respondents would not care if people knew what they thought on these topics. It is probably best to provide anonymity if you can because no one has shown that promising anonymity produces worse response rates. Even when the data are anonymous, you still must follow the other procedures described above in which you do not leave questionnaires lying around for idle eyes to view and in which you do not report data for small groups of respondents.

Reminders

Probably the single most important technique to use to produce high response rates is to send out reminders (Denton, Tsai, & Chevrette, 1988; Dillman, Carpenter, Christenson, & Brooks, 1974; Eckland, 1965; Etzel & Walker, 1974; Filion, 1976; Ford & Zeisel, 1949; Furse, Stewart, & Rados, 1981; House, Gerber, & McMichael, 1977; Jones & Lang, 1980; Kanuk & Berenson, 1975; Kephart & Bressler, 1958; Linsky, 1975; Yammarino et al., 1991). Even under the best of circumstances you will not achieve acceptable levels of returns if you do not send out any reminders. Actually, it is important to send out several reminders, and it is important to pay attention to the timing of the reminders.

If you carefully keep track of the daily returns that you get, an interesting pattern unfolds. For the first few days after you mail out the questionnaires you get nothing back. This makes sense because it takes time for a survey to be delivered, it takes a short period to fill it out, and then a day or two to get it back to you in the mail (actually this can be a day or two longer if you use business reply returns). About 5 to 7 days after you send out the initial mailing you begin to get a few back; then in the next few days you get a lot more back, with more coming in each day than the day before. Around the 10th day after your mailing, the returns start to level off, and then around the 14th day they start dropping off precipitously.

This drop-off in returns is a signal that whatever motivational influence your initial letter had is now fading. Respondents who have not returned questionnaires by now are going to begin to forget doing it, or they are going to misplace the survey under a pile of things on their desk. You want to plan your first reminder to arrive at the respondents' addresses just at this point in the return pattern, at about the 14th day.

After sending out a reminder, we then see the same pattern repeating itself: A few days of no impact, then a burst of returns with more coming in each day, and then a precipitous decline at about 14 days after the second mailing (the 1st reminder).

The other interesting feature about this return pattern is that whatever return rate you got in the first wave (e.g., 40%), you will get about half that amount in the second wave (e.g., 20%). Figure 6.1 shows this pattern very clearly. These were the return rates for six different companies to which we sent mail questionnaires to managers asking their opinions about work-related alcohol policies and problems at their worksites. As you can see, the overall response rates were very good (exceeding 80% for each company), and in each round of reminders we received back about half the amount that we had received from the previous round.

Therefore, because I recommend shooting for at least a 75% return rate, you should plan on at least four mailings—the initial mailing and then three reminders. Each of these mailings should be spaced about two weeks apart. This should give you approximately the following pattern of returns: 40% + 20% + 10% + 5% = 75%. This means that your total mailing period will take about 8 to 9 weeks because you have to leave time after your last reminder for the returns to come in. Sending reminders out sooner than two weeks does not speed up the returns. All it does is send reminders to people who were going to do it anyway.

Spreading two or three reminders out over a longer time (to save money on postage) is not as effective in producing a good return rate. You do not keep building momentum among the nonresponders with your reminders because the gap in time is so long that they have forgotten about the survey. Each reminder has to start all over again in getting people to decide to participate.

What is also interesting about this pattern is that the rate of returns and the number of reminders have nothing to do with the total size of your sample. You follow the same procedures whether your sample size is 200 or 20,000. The only impact on size is that you have to have a bigger staff of people to help you get out the mailings each round.

% of Returns

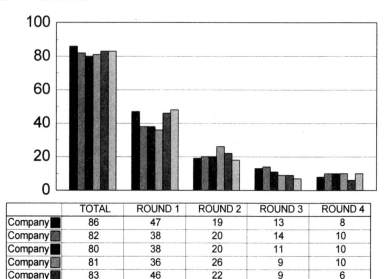

	TOTAL	ROUND 1	ROUND 2	ROUND 3	ROUND 4
Company ■	86	47	19	13	8
Company ▨	82	38	20	14	10
Company ■	80	38	20	11	10
Company ▦	81	36	26	9	10
Company ▨	83	46	22	9	6
Company ▢	83	48	18	7	10

Figure 6.1. Proportion Returned by Rounds of Mailings for Six Companies

What should you put in each mailing? Is each mailing just a repeat of the first mailing? No. I recommend sending a complete package (respondent letter, questionnaire, return envelope) in the first and third mailings. In the second and fourth mailings I believe you can limit yourself to a postcard or letter reminder.

In each of the four mailings, the letter addressed to the respondent should focus on slightly different issues. For the first mailing you want to be the most thorough, covering all the bases. In the second mailing you want to be gentle and friendly. "Just a reminder in case you haven't yet sent in your questionnaire. We would really like to hear from you." In the third mailing you want to emphasize the confidentiality of responses and the importance of getting a good return so that all points of view are represented. You should also note that you are including another copy of the questionnaire in case they misplaced the first one you sent. The fourth mailing should be a "last call." Set a specific deadline and encourage people to send in their questionnaire so that their points of view can be represented.

If you are using a procedure that promises confidentiality, then you can keep track of the questionnaires being returned by placing a code number on the survey form and then sending out reminders only to people from whom you have not yet received questionnaires. This saves you money on postage, printing, and supplies and keeps respondents from being annoyed (or confused) by receiving reminders after they have already sent in their surveys.

If you want a procedure that gives the respondents anonymity, then the steps to follow are a little more complicated. Because you do not know who has sent back their questionnaire and who has not, you have two alternate strategies for producing reminders. The first method is to send reminders to everybody and always include a line that says "If you've already sent in your questionnaire, thank you very much." You probably also want to say, "Because your returns are anonymous we don't know which of you have sent in your questionnaires and which of you have not, so that is why we are sending this reminder to everyone." I personally do not like to use this strategy because (a) it is wasteful of postage, supplies, and resources; (b) it irritates respondents to get reminders when they have returned their questionnaires; (c) it confuses them and sometimes leads to respondents worrying that their survey got lost in the mail, so that they fill out a second one that you do not want but cannot remove from the pile because you do not know if it is someone's second questionnaire; and (d) it dilutes your reminder letters because some of the verbiage is apologizing to people who have already returned their questionnaires and not just focusing on those who have yet to return them.

I prefer a second strategy that I call the "reminder postcard strategy." This strategy enables you to accomplish two things at once: It maintains complete anonymity for the respondents' returned questionnaires while also letting you know who has and has not returned the questionnaire. This lets you send reminders only to those who have yet to respond. The way to accomplish this is to enclose a postage-paid, return postcard that *does* have either an identification code or the person's name (or both) on it. The instructions tell the respondent explicitly that returning this postcard tells us that they do not need any reminders. You also instruct them to mail the postcard back *separately* from the questionnaire. By using this procedure you know who has returned the questionnaire without having to put any identifying information on the questionnaire itself. Figure 6.2 shows an example of this type of postcard.

The first thing researchers worry about is "what if the respondent just sends back the postcard and not the questionnaire." That would be a

This is to let you know that I have returned my questionnaire and that you no longer need to send me any reminders.

> Label with Respondent's Name
> and
> ID Number on it

.

.

.

     Your answers to this survey will be anonymous because there is no name or identification number on the questionnaire. After you return your questionnaire to us, send separately the enclosed postcard. That will tell us that you don't need any reminders, while at the same time maintaining your anonymity. Thank you for your efforts.

Figure 6.2. Sample of Postcard and Associated Paragraph in Respondent Letter

problem, but it turns out that it is not the case. You usually get more questionnaires back than postcards. Some respondents forget to mail their postcards, some lose them, and some purposely do not send them back as a way of ensuring their anonymity. These latter folks are willing to put up with getting reminders they do not need to guarantee their anonymity. Thankfully there are only a few who take this route (e.g., 5% or so), or else the method would not achieve its intended purpose of providing you information about who has responded while maintaining anonymity.

What If You Cannot Afford to Do Follow-Ups?

Many times researchers choose to do mail surveys because they are on a very limited budget, and therefore the suggestion to do four mailings conflicts with budgetary constraints. Also, researchers may be under time pressure to get the survey results quickly and therefore feel that they cannot afford the time that it takes to do four mailings.

Researchers in this bind sometimes fall into the trap of creating a survey design that provides for a large sample that gets only one mailing without any reminders, and settling for the 30% to 40% return rate. They still wind up with enough surveys to analyze because of the large sample. These researchers draw comfort from having 1000 questionnaires returned because the sampling error formula says that the amount of sampling error for a sample of 1000 is relatively small. The fallacy in this thinking is that somehow a bigger number of questionnaires that represents a 30% return rate is more valid than a smaller number of questionnaires that represents a 30% return rate. Unfortunately both circumstances produce flawed surveys because we can never be certain that the 30% who responded accurately represent the whole population.

So how does the researcher who has budgetary and time constraints deal with these conflicting pressures? As a fall-back method I recommend sending follow-ups to a random subset of your overall sample. What does this accomplish? It provides a way of testing to what extent your low response rate returners are different from a "true" random subset on *all* of the variables measured in your study while at the same time not costing as much as sending reminders to everyone.

To set up this mechanism you need to divide your original sample into two groups: One group (presumably the larger of the two) will be designated to get fewer reminders (in order to save money and time) and the other group (the smaller) will get the full arsenal of techniques.

You need to distinguish the two groups in your code numbers so that you can (a) keep track of the different return rates and (b) analyze the data separately for the two groups.

When you are ready to begin your analyses, you compare the lower responding group to the higher responding group's answers. You hope to find no differences, or only a few unimportant differences, in the two groups. If this is so, you can present the data from your low responding group with the full confidence that it is "representative" of the whole sample even though you obtained a low response rate. In other words, the choice of whether to respond or not was not correlated with the answers to your questions. The nonresponders looked just like the responders.

Things get a little bit more complicated if there are differences. How you deal with the situation depends on the extent of the differences. If there are a few sharp differences between the low responding sample and the high responding sample, then the easiest thing to do is to report the findings on these few characteristics based only on the high responding group. For instance, if there were differences in the proportion of males who were included in the high and low responding groups, you would describe the gender distribution of your population based on the findings from the high response group.

If, however, you find out that the group that is underrepresented also gives different answers to the rest of the questions, then additional corrections must be made. One strategy is to present your findings on these other answers separately for the over- and underrepresented groups (for example by males and females). Another strategy is to force your data to mirror the "correct" proportion of males and females (and hence also represent the correct mix of male and female answers to the rest of your questions). You do this by weighting your data in such a way that the underrepresented group is restored to its proper proportion of the overall sample. This procedure "assumes" that the males who did respond were like the males who did not respond, and the only thing you need to adjust is the proportion of males in the total sample.

Because you have complete information on a small subset, you are actually in a good position to test out this assumption by comparing the answers of males in the low responding group to the answers of the males in the high responding group. If they are similar, then the assumption holds.

If the answers between the low responding subsample and the high responding subsample are different on a variety of indicators, then you are stuck. You have clearly shown that your responding sample is not a representative group. You may have to relent and try to scrape together enough extra resources to send reminders to the rest of the non-responding sample. In the worst case you would try to publish your report with a lot of caveats about the nonrepresentativeness of the returns.

Length of the Questionnaire

It almost goes without saying that you are likely to get a better response rate with a shorter questionnaire than with a longer one. Within this general recommendation, the real world is a little more compli-cated. It turns out that there are no clear demarcation points. It is not like a 12-page questionnaire will get a decent response rate but a 13-page questionnaire will not. There has been a fair amount of research on this issue, but the results are muddled because of several confound-ing factors (Berdie, 1973; Burchell & Marsh, 1992; Champion & Sear, 1969; Childers & Ferrell, 1979; Lockhart, 1991; Mason et al., 1961; Roscoe, Lang, & Sheth, 1975; Scott, 1961).

Part of the confusion has to do with how we measure the length of the questionnaire. Are we talking about the number of questions, are we referring to the number of pages, or are we talking about some combination of the two? (Thirty questions on 3 pages may seem differ-ent from 30 questions on 6 pages.) Another confounder is that different length questionnaires may be perceived differently in terms of interest levels or in terms of importance. Longer questionnaires may actually be seen as more interesting or more important because they can get a fuller picture of a topic than a more cursory version. Even within one meth-odological study to test the effects of varying questionnaire length, it is hard to "hold constant" such other factors that may play a role in response rates. Many studies that try hard to control these issues wind up comparing different length questionnaires that are actually not that different. For example, a study by Adams and Gale (1982) made com-parisons of surveys with 1 versus 3 pages versus 5 pages. They found no difference in response rates between one and three pages but did find a lower response rate for 5 pages.

In addition, drawing conclusions from findings on a series of studies is difficult because they each have differences in topics covered, sam-ple, reminder procedures, and so on. An ambitious review by Heberlein and Baumgartner (1978) that covered 98 methodological studies was unable to document any zero order correlation between length measures and overall responses.

The message to take away from this is that length by itself is not the sole determining factor that decides response rates. No matter what the length, other design factors can influence whether a good response rate is obtained or not. Within a specific design, however, I believe shorter questionnaires will on average do better than substantially longer versions.

From my experience, I think the real issue for the researcher is to design a questionnaire that *efficiently* asks about all the elements that are important to the study. You want to avoid series of questions that seem off the topic; you want to avoid questions that are redundant; you want to avoid unnecessarily long sequences of questions that try to measure very minor differences in issues (e.g., asking about the actual length of time you had to wait in a doctor's waiting room, plus how long you had to wait in the examining room before the doctor came in, plus asking overall how long of a wait you had, plus asking how satisfied you were with the waiting time). There are also important issues of presentation and layout that can affect the perceived length of the questionnaire. These will be described in the next chapter.

Clarity of Instructions

Another factor that contributes to perceived respondent burden and that in turn affects response rates is the clarity of the instructions that are part of the questionnaire. It is not surprising to find that forms that have complicated or confusing or wrong instructions create frustration for respondents and that the result of this frustration is a failure to return the questionnaire.

Instructions should be precise, short, and clearly visible. In addition, various format aids such as boldface type or boxing or arrows to supplement written directions help the respondent to comply with instructions. Figure 6.3 shows an example of trying to make instructions clear. The purpose is stated at the top of the page; the skip instructions are listed in all capital letters for categories #9 and #10 of question #1; and the definition of a "drink" is put in a box at question #2. In addition, it helps to use someone who has a graphical perspective to review the layout of your questionnaire. We will discuss these issues in more detail in Chapter 8.

Respondent Motivation

In discussing the techniques to produce higher response rates in this chapter, we have alluded to various respondent motivations. It is useful,

━━━━━━━━━━ SECTION H ━━━━━━━━━━

Individual Background Characteristics

———————

These questions are being asked only so that we can compare answers of different groups of managers/supervisors. No data will be released to anyone that would <u>ever</u> allow identification of an individual.

1. Considering <u>all</u> of your drinking behavior in the past 30 days, about how often did you have any beer, wine, or liquor to drink?

1   Three or more times a day

2   Twice a day

3   Once a day

4   Nearly every day (five or six days a week)

5   Two to four days a week

6   Once a week

7   Three days a month

8   One or two days a month

9   Not at all in past month, but I do drink (SKIP TO Q5)

10   Not at all, because I don't drink (SKIP TO Q5)

2. In the past 30 days, on a <u>typical day</u> that you drank, about how much did you have to drink in a day?

> One "drink" means:
>
> a 12-ounce can or bottle of beer or
> a 4-ounce glass of wine or
> a 12-ounce wine cooler or
> a 1-ounce shot glass of liquor or
> spirits, alone or in a mixed drink.

1   One drink

2   Two drinks

3   Three drinks

4   Four drinks

5   Five drinks

6   Six drinks

7   Seven drinks

8   Eight or more drinks

3. In the past 30 days, what was the <u>most</u> you had to drink <u>on any one day</u>?

1   One drink

2   Two drinks

3   Three drinks

4   Four drinks

5   Five drinks

6   Six drinks

7   Seven drinks

8   Eight drinks

9   Nine drinks

10   Ten or more drinks

4. How many days in the past 30 days did you drink that much?

1   One day

2   Two or three days

3   Four to seven days

4   Eight to thirteen days

5   Fourteen to twenty days

6   More than twenty days

5. How do your drinking patterns during the <u>last three years</u> compare to what they were <u>previously</u>?

1   Drinking more now

2   Drinking less now

3   No change

———

12

Figure 6.3. Example of Formatting for Instructions: Alcohol Sequence in Policy Questionnaire

however, to be more specific about these motivational patterns so that as you choose among your techniques you can do so with an eye toward procedures that will help respondents decide to participate.

People do not want to spend their time doing things that are not useful, not interesting, or painful. If people think that participating in a study will accomplish something useful, then they are motivated to follow through and complete the survey. The primary mechanism to create the sense of usefulness is the respondent letter. Usually one or two paragraphs are all you devote to this part of the letter, so you can see how important it is that these paragraphs are well written. To the extent that you can articulate how this survey will directly affect the respondents' lives, you will go a long way toward convincing the respondent that completing the questionnaire is a useful process.

Making your questionnaire interesting has a lot to do with the topics you choose to ask about, but it also depends on how the questions are put together, including formatting and sequencing. Pretesting and literature reviews will help you to focus on those questions that provide the information you need and also are easy for respondents to relate to. Pretesting will also give you feedback on questions for which the formatting causes problems or confusion. You want to alter the question format in any way necessary to make it easy for respondents to use the questionnaire. The flow of the questionnaire can make it seem more interesting to the extent that the questions are ordered in logical sequences and relevant groupings of issues. There is no one way to do this; taking a crack at it and then making improvements in response to feedback is the best way to accomplish this goal.

It also is common sense that respondents will not want to fill out a questionnaire if it is painful—either immediately in the sense that it is an ordeal to fill out or delayed in the sense that they fear something bad will happen to them because they filled out the questionnaire. Again clarity and logical flow go a long way toward solving the immediate pain issue. Using grammatically correct and unambiguous terms reduces immediate pain.

Staying true to your promises of confidentiality or anonymity is the primary mechanism to protect respondents from any delayed pain. You also need to be careful in how the data are analyzed and reported to ensure that no harm comes to respondents. Primarily this means presenting data for large groups of people and being careful to mask institutional affiliations. For instance, you would not say: "Respondents who joined the health club after January 1 were unanimous in denouncing the management of the club." By reporting this finding in that way, you have broken the shield of confidentiality that you promised respondents.

The final issue to keep in mind about respondents participating in a mail survey is that the action needed from the respondents is not that high on their list of priorities. There are lots of things in people's lives that may seem more important or pressing than getting around to completing your questionnaire. That is why it is so important to plan a process that includes reminders and that the timing of reminders keeps the momentum up as the respondent finally reaches the action point of finishing the questionnaire and putting it in the mail to you.

7

Additional Ways to Reduce Nonresponse Errors

In this chapter we want to discuss additional strategies that you can use to reduce the nonresponse rate in your surveys. There are a variety of mechanisms that you can use, and using as many of them as feasible should be your goal. We will also discuss some ideas that in some situations have proven beneficial but other times have not shown themselves to be effective. Obviously, you will want to assess whether you believe these strategies will help in your particular situation.

INCENTIVES

Other than follow-up reminders, there is no technique more likely to improve your response rate than incentives. It turns out, however, that the research findings hold some surprises as we consider various options in providing incentives to respondents. The logic of an incentive is simple: Raise the stakes explicitly for the respondents by giving them something in return for filling out the questionnaire. The differences come in when we try to figure out what to give to the respondents and when to give it to them.

Logically one would assume that you would send the respondents a reward after they returned the questionnaire, and you would let the respondents know in the respondent letter that this was the deal. More respondents would be motivated to participate because of the promise of this reward. Obviously, the respondent would have to value whatever it was that you were offering, or else it would not have any motivational value. One disadvantage with this mechanism is that respondents receive a delayed reward; they get their reward several weeks (probably) after their "good" behavior.

Another possibility would be to offer the reward in advance, including it with the mailing in anticipation of the respondents' participation. The advantage here is that the impact is immediate; the respondent gets the benefit right away. We should not underestimate the motivational power of the implied contract: "They gave me this reward, so I had better do my part by filling out the questionnaire or else I wouldn't be living up to my end of the bargain." The disadvantage here (both financially and morally) is that some people get the reward but do not deserve it because they do not return the surveys anyway. Because of this problem, one goal in using this technique is to figure out the least value of the reward that you need to give in order to achieve the effects that you want.

Monetary Rewards

The simplest and most direct reward is to give people money. There have been a variety of studies and reviews of the literature that show that if you offer monetary incentives, your response rate will be improved (Armstrong, 1975; Brennan, Hoek, & Astridge, 1991; Church, 1993; Dommeyer, 1988; Duncan, 1979; Fox, Crask, & Kim, 1988; Friedman & San Augustine, 1979; Heberlein & Baumgartner, 1978; Hopkins & Gullickson, 1992; Huck & Gleason, 1974; Kanuk & Berenson, 1975; Linsky, 1975; Scott, 1961; Yammarino, Skinner, & Childers, 1991; Yu & Cooper, 1983). What is also clear from this research is that prepaid monetary incentives are more effective than promised monetary rewards (Blumberg, Fuller, & Hare, 1974; Cox, 1976; Hancock, 1940; O'Keefe & Homer, 1987; Schewe & Cournoyer, 1976; Wotruba, 1966). There have been contradictory conclusions drawn about the impact of promised monetary rewards compared to no rewards, but there are examples of studies that have shown benefits for promised rewards although they are not as great as prepaid rewards (Yu & Cooper, 1983).

What is surprising about these research results is that it does not seem to take a very big reward to stimulate an improved response rate. Many studies are reported in the literature that show the benefits of $.25 and $.50! However, many of these studies were done 15 to 20 years ago. It seems important to extrapolate the findings from these studies to the "current" value of the dollar. The review by Hopkins and Gullickson (1992) equated these values to 1990 dollars and still showed improvements for values less than $.50.

The question about whether there are increasing benefits for increasing dollar amounts is harder to answer definitively. It turns out that much of the experimentation that has been done to test alternate amounts have not tended to use dollar amounts more than $1, therefore, the number of studies we have available to make generalizations about larger sized incentives is relatively few. The review by Hopkins and Gullickson (1992) did show an increasing percentage of improvement over "no incentive" control methods for greater incentive values, but the top group was designated as $2 or more and included only eight studies.

Another point that speaks to the issue of whether larger rewards (e.g., $5) or smaller rewards (e.g., $1) are better has to do with our understanding of the meaning of the reward to the respondent. With small amounts of money people clearly do *not* interpret the reward as a fair market exchange for their time. Even a $1 reward for filling out a 20-minute questionnaire works out to only a $3 per hour rate of pay. Therefore, people must view the reward in another light; one idea is that it represents to the respondent a token of good faith or a "trust builder" (Dillman, 1978). The respondent feels that the research staff is nice to show their appreciation by giving the incentive and therefore feels motivated to reciprocate by filling out the questionnaire.

According to this perspective, then, the problem with giving a larger reward such as $5 is that now the amount does approach fair market value for people's time. For instance, $5 for filling out a 20-minute questionnaire is equivalent to $15 an hour. Now the reward looks like a real job (even if a short-lived one), and the respondent thinks, "I'm being offered this job, do I want to do it? Maybe not." So in a funny way, the larger the reward, the more the respondent is free to view it as a job offer and feel free to decline the job.

There is another psychological theory called cognitive dissonance theory that gives a slightly different interpretation about why larger amounts may not be better than smaller amounts. According to this theory, the respondent might conclude that there is something wrong with the study if the researchers have to pay someone so much money to fill it out. If that is their viewpoint, then they would be justified in not participating even if they kept the money. The smaller amounts of money used as a reward work in the opposite fashion and therefore support the notion that this is an important study (Hackler & Bourgette, 1973).

Just to give this theorizing a touch of reality, there have been a few studies that do report providing larger sized rewards, and it looks like response rates for larger rewards tend to be higher than for those with smaller rewards (Hopkins & Gullickson, 1992; James & Bolstein, 1992; Yu & Cooper, 1983). In particular, higher incentive amounts are reported in the literature when conducting surveys of persons in professional occupations, particularly doctors. Incentive amounts from $20 to $25 to $50 have been used (Godwin, 1979). In these circumstances, higher response rates are obtained with higher rewards (Berry & Kanouse, 1987). In addition, my own experience with our recent nonexperimental study dealing with alcohol use and work had one worksite in which we used a $5 upfront incentive. The resulting response rate was 82%.

One final point about monetary incentives and their desired effects is that the key to effectiveness seems to be creating a climate in which the prepaid incentive is seen as a feel-good thing rather than as a manipulative technique to coerce the respondent into participation.

Another variation on the idea of monetary rewards is using a "lottery" prize structure. This technique falls within the "promised reward" category, but with a twist. Respondents are offered a "chance" at a "big" prize, although they also have, of course, a chance of getting nothing. Again, research on this variation is limited, so that definitive generalizations about its effectiveness are not possible (Hopkins & Gullickson, 1992; Gajraj, Faria, & Dickinson, 1990; Lorenzi, Friedmann, & Paolillo, 1988). The logic behind this idea is that the chance of hitting big will be such an inducement that respondents will fill out their surveys to qualify. This technique also works well if you are trying to encourage respondents to mail in their surveys by a particular deadline.

The other issue that must be dealt with if you want to use this technique is anonymity, or rather the lack of it. In order to have a drawing and give out prizes, you need to know the name and address associated with each returned survey. This lack of anonymity may be counterproductive in some circumstances. The "postcard" mechanism that we discussed in the previous chapter provides a solution to this dilemma. The surveys themselves are returned anonymously, but the postcards have the respondents' names and addresses on them. To be eligible for the lottery, the postcard would need to be returned.

It seems like enterprising respondents would realize that all they really have to do to be eligible for the lottery is to turn in their postcard. You would not really be able to tell whether they actually sent in their questionnaires. It seems that the more attractive the "prize," the more motivation there would be to cheat. However, respondents do not seem to do that. My recent experience with this technique in 12 different worksites across the county showed that we never received more postcards back than we did questionnaires, even though we were offering three $250 lottery prizes at each worksite.

Nonmonetary Rewards

Of course it is possible to reward respondents with other things besides money (Brennan, 1958; Furse & Stewart, 1982; Hansen, 1980; Nederhof, 1983). All sorts of things have been, and can be, used—ball point pens, cups, movie tickets, and so on. The logic of giving a "gift" is similar to that for giving a token amount of money. The idea is to express to the respondent that you are appreciative of their efforts and want to thank them for their participation. Again, like money rewards it is possible to think about the gift being given as a "prepaid" gift or as a "promised" gift that is sent after the survey is returned (Brennan, 1958; Pucel, Nelson, & Wheeler, 1971).

There has not been as much research on the differences between prepaid versus promised gifts but one would assume that the effectiveness would follow the same pattern as with monetary rewards—prepaid gifts would probably have a better effect. Also, there has not been much research done on the "value" of the gift to see what the trends are with more valuable gifts. To some extent the concept of value is less obvious with many types of gifts. Also, it is possible that the gift's perceived value exceeds the actual cost of the gift itself. This could arise because respondents may not have a good sense about how much such a gift costs, or it may be because by buying in bulk you can get a discount. Movie passes are great in this regard because they cost you only about $4 although they are good at movies that cost about $7 normally.

Other Incentives

Sometimes respondents can be offered other incentives that encourage them to respond (Dommeyer, 1985; Hubbard & Little, 1988). These alternate devices will provide improvements in response rates to the extent that the offer is viewed as valuable by respondents. I recently had occasion to be part of a survey study in which respondents were asked to fill out a short questionnaire concerning their nutritional intake. The researchers also needed respondents to include a clipping from their toenails! As an incentive, respondents were told that when they returned the survey they would receive a detailed nutritional analysis of their own diet based on their report and their toenail clippings. Returns were over 70% with only one reminder.

Another interesting incentive is to offer a contribution to a charity in the respondents' names if surveys are returned (Robertson & Bellenger, 1978). Obviously the perceived value of the charity might have some impact on its effectiveness. This technique can be used on an individual basis or group basis. The individual strategy would be to contribute a certain amount (say $5) to a charity for each survey returned. Specific charities can be designated, or you can allow respondents to check off among a few offerings, or you can ask them to write in their own suggestions. The group strategy would provide a significant payment to a charity if the sample as a whole provided a certain number or percentage of returns (e.g., a 70% return rate). My recent worksite study included two sites in which we used the group strategy, a $750 contribution to charity, and wound up with response rates of 68% and 78%.

Incentives Versus Reminders

Now that we have extolled the virtues of incentives as well as reminders, a legitimate question is whether incentives should be used instead of reminders. The question can be answered from the perspective of final response rates, cost effectiveness, and quickness of returns. A study by James and Bolstein (1990) gives some information on this issue. They ran an experiment using different amounts of incentives (none, $.25, $.50, $1, and $2) and kept track of the response rates at the end of each of the four mailings using a four-page questionnaire. The highest rates of returns were provided by using both methods in combination—four mailings and a $2 prepaid incentive. This strategy is also the most expensive. Good return rates (although a little lower than the combination method) were also obtained by using two mailings and a $2 incentive or four mailings and no incentive. The no incentive strategy was slightly less expensive than the incentive strategy but of course it took more time for the additional waves of mailings to be administered. If time rather than money is the limiting factor, then using incentives may allow you to save some time; if money is the limiting factor then planning for multiple mailings with no incentives may be the best. If a high response rate is the major goal, then multiple mailings and incentives should be used together.

OTHER TECHNIQUES

There are other techniques beyond reminders and incentives that have been shown to improve response rates. Some techniques show consistent improvements; some have shown improvements in only some circumstances.

Prenotification

One interesting variation of the reminder mechanism is to prenotify respondents before they receive the survey. In a sense this is a reminder done ahead of time. Basically it is a contact by mail or phone that "warns" the respondent that they have been selected to be in a survey and to keep an eye open for its arrival in the mail a week or two in the future. The impact of the prenotification is generally equivalent to one reminder (Allen, Schewe, & Wijk, 1980; Brunner & Carroll, 1969; Ford, 1967; Furse, Stewart, & Rados, 1981; Heaton, 1965; Jolson, 1977; Kerin & Peterson, 1977; Myers & Haug, 1969; Parsons & Medford, 1972; Schegelmilch & Diamantopoulos, 1991; Stafford, 1966; Walker & Burdick, 1977; Wynn & McDaniel, 1985; Yammarino et al., 1991).

This procedure provides one way to shorten the interval from the first mailing of the survey until the last reminder. You can "gain" 2 weeks on your return schedule by mailing out the prenotification letter a couple of weeks before you send out the questionnaire. You would send it out about the same time that the questionnaire goes off to the printer.

Return Postage

It almost goes without saying that paying for the return postage will increase response rates. Maybe because this is such an obvious procedure, there have not been all that many studies that explicitly test this assertion. The few that have been done certainly confirm this point (Armstrong & Lusk, 1987; Blumberg et al., 1974; Ferris, 1951; Harris & Guffey, 1978; McCrohan & Lowe, 1981; Price, 1950; Yammarino et al., 1991).

There has been more research on the type of postage put on the return envelope. The alternatives are to use some kind of business reply franking or to put a stamp on the return envelope. The advantage of the business reply is that you get charged only for questionnaires that are actually returned. By the way, the post office does charge a little extra for this service, something on the order of magnitude of $.07 per returned questionnaire. This "extra" cost needs to be factored in when comparing the costs of alternate postage mechanisms. The disadvantage of this choice is that it gives more of the appearance of impersonality.

The alternate procedure of putting a stamp on the return envelope seems to produce a small increase in return rates (Brook, 1978; Jones & Linda, 1978; Kimball, 1961; Watson, 1965). The reason for this is that respondents do not want to "waste" the stamp by not returning the questionnaire and yet are not crass enough to peel it off and use it for their own purposes. We are using the value put on avoiding wastefulness to induce a better response rate. There have also been some studies that show using pretty commemorative type stamps has a slight advantage over regular stamps (Henley, 1976; Jones & Linda, 1978; Martin & McConnell, 1970). The disadvantage of this approach is its cost. Not only do you "pay" for stamps that ultimately never get used but it also costs time and money to get the stamps, lick them (the post office now offers self-stick stamps in some denominations), and stick them on all the envelopes.

Outgoing Postage

The usual alternatives for types of outgoing postage are stamps or metered mail using a postage meter. There have been a few studies done that show a slight advantage for stamps, particular commemorative stamps, on outgoing envelopes (Blumenfeld, 1973; Dillman, 1972; Hopkins & Podolak, 1983; Kernan, 1971; McCrohan & Lowe, 1981; Peterson, 1975; Vocino, 1977). The explanation for this difference is that respondents are less likely to assume the mailing is "junk mail" if there is a stamp on the envelope and therefore actually open the envelope. The only disadvantage for stamps again is the extra cost of sticking them on the envelopes.

There is a third postage option. It is called a first class indicia. It is like the business reply except that it is used for outgoing first class mail. You print your account number and a first class designation on your outgoing envelopes. The post office keeps track of your mailings and deducts the postage amounts from a prepaid account that you have set up with them. This is the least labor intensive method of sending out your questionnaires, but it probably suffers somewhat from the same problem as metered mail in that it may be confused with "junk mail."

There has also been some research on the value of using premium postage for mailings such as special delivery or next day delivery services. The research shows there to be some advantage for this type of postage, but the costs are so substantial that many consider this prohibitive (Clausen & Ford, 1947; Kephart & Bressler, 1958). When special postage is used, it is most often used for the final reminders. At least you are mailing to only part of your sample at this stage.

Study Sponsorship

Respondents are more likely to respond to surveys that they consider important or prestigious (Doob, Freedman, & Carlsmith, 1973; Houston & Nevin, 1977; Jones & Lang, 1980; Jones & Linda, 1978; Peterson, 1975; Roeher, 1963; Watson, 1965). Therefore they are more likely to respond to surveys that are sponsored by government agencies or well-known universities (Houston & Nevin, 1977; Jones & Lang, 1980; Jones & Linda, 1978; Peterson, 1975). Also, perhaps they are less concerned that the survey is a ploy to sell them real estate or insurance if it comes on university or government agency letterhead.

Color of the Questionnaire

There have been a few studies that show that the color of the questionnaire cover affects return rates (Gullahorn & Gullahorn, 1963; Pressley & Tullar, 1977; Pucel et al., 1971). The explanation for this effect is that a color other than white might stand out more on the respondent's desk so the respondent is less apt to misplace it or to forget to deal with it. Green versus white are the colors that have been tested most often; the relative values of colors other than green have not been tested to any large extent.

ADDITIONAL TECHNIQUES TO CONSIDER

There are a variety of other techniques that have not consistently shown improvements in response rates but that have from time to time shown an impact. Unfortunately it is hard to know when these might have a positive effect and when they might not. Using them is riskier, therefore, at least in terms of ensuring positive results. On the other hand, for most, using it will not hurt.

Types of Appeal

When you write your cover letter and you come to the paragraph that speaks to why the respondent should participate, there are several different approaches that could be taken. You can use the scientific approach—"our sample won't be valid unless everyone responds." You can use the egoistic approach—"this is how participating will benefit you." You can use the social utility approach—"this study is important and worthwhile." None of these approaches has consistently proved better than the others (Bachman, 1987; Childers, Pride, & Ferrell, 1980; Hendrick, Borden, Giesen, Murray, & Seyfried, 1972; Houston & Nevin, 1977; Yammarino et al., 1991; Yu & Cooper, 1983).

Personalization

A closely related technique is personalization, either through the salutation to the respondent by using a name as opposed to a more anonymous greeting such as "dear Boston resident," or by personally signed letters. Neither procedure has consistently shown benefits for response rates (Andreasen, 1970; Carpenter, 1975; Dillman & Frey, 1974; Frazier & Bird, 1958; Houston & Jefferson, 1975; Kawash & Aleamoni, 1971; Kerin & Peterson, 1977; Kimball, 1961; Rucker, Hughes, Thompson, Harrison, & Vanderlip, 1984; Simon, 1967; Weilbacher & Walsh, 1952). Some authors have commented that by personalizing the letters you may have just the opposite effect by calling attention to the fact that you know the respondent's name.

Deadlines

Providing the respondents with a deadline for responding has a nice appeal to it. The presumption is that respondents would try harder to return the questionnaire by the deadline, rather than putting it aside for a while and then forgetting it. The use of a deadline gets a little complicated when you are also using reminders. You do not want to say that 2 weeks from now is the deadline for responding, and then send the respondent a reminder at that time saying "please respond, we're giving you 2 more weeks." On the other hand, you do not want to give a deadline of 8 weeks in the future, because that hardly serves any motivating purposes.

What research has been done on the use of deadlines does not show any particular advantage in final response rates. What it does show is that the returns come in a little faster (Futrell & Hise, 1982; Henley, 1976; Kanuk & Berenson, 1975; Linsky, 1975; Nevin & Ford, 1976; Roberts, McCrory, & Forthofer, 1978; Vocino, 1977). My suggestion is to use soft deadlines that also incorporate the information about subsequent reminders, such as "Please try to respond within the next week, so we won't have to send you any reminders."

8

The Benefits of Aesthetics and Good Management

In this chapter we will address a variety of issues that transform a mail survey from a "good" product to an "excellent" product. Many of these elements are seemingly small points, but they go a long way toward making the study efficient, which in turn can affect the overall effectiveness of the effort, hold down costs, and improve the quality of the data. These issues fall into two broad categories—management issues and aesthetics.

MANAGEMENT

Because the mail survey process does not involve a staff of interviewers that need to be hired, trained, and supervised, researchers sometimes overlook the importance of managing the research process. There are three areas of management that need to be attended to—designing a good schedule, incorporating a good quality control system, and defining roles.

The Schedule

Having a clear, precise, and written schedule will aid you immeasurably in the management of the mail survey process. The schedule will enable you to appreciate how the various parts of the mail survey study have to fit together like a jigsaw puzzle to carry out the project in a timely fashion. By having a schedule you are also able to anticipate issues so that you are not overly rushed to get a particular step accomplished. It also serves as a checklist to ensure that you have not forgotten something.

In making up a schedule, you have to recognize that there are really several independent processes that come together to make a mail survey study. These processes include the sampling process, the development of the questionnaire, the development of other materials, the printing of the questionnaire (and other materials), the data collection period, and the coding and data entry process.

People have different preferences about how to construct a schedule. Some people like to start at the end—when the results are due—and work backward toward the start date. This assumes that the time window to conduct the study is fixed, and time is to be allocated among the various phases of the study within this fixed period. As components are allocated portions of time, those with fixed periods of time are entered into the schedule first. For example, we know that the data collection period is predetermined after you decide how many reminders you are going to send out and exactly how long you are going to wait between reminders. If you choose to do an original mailing and then three reminders with two weeks between mailings, then the data collection process will take eight to nine weeks.

Another common fixed period is how long it will take the printer to print the number of copies of the questionnaire that you need, encompassing the period from the day you give it to the printer until the day that the surveys are delivered to you.

By using this mechanism to build your schedule, you then allocate the remaining time to the other phases of the study. Inevitably, some phases begin to get scrunched for time. You may discover that you have only 2 weeks to develop your questionnaire, or you may find that you have a only 3-week period after the last questionnaire arrives to code, analyze, and write up your report.

One way to deal with this scarcity of time is to overlap various functions in your schedule. For instance, you can be producing your sample while you are developing your questionnaire. Also, you can begin the coding and data entry process even while questionnaires are still coming in.

An alternate way to construct a schedule is to start at the beginning of the project and to allocate time to various phases based on your estimates of the time you will need. Again for some phases you can be more certain about how much time they will take; others will require some educated guesses. As you get more experience you will become better at estimating how long each phase may require.

As you put together your schedule, it is a very good policy to leave some time in the schedule for unexpected issues or slippage when something does not go exactly as planned. Sometimes the printer does not come through by the date promised or sometimes you decide that you really want to pretest a particular section of troublesome questions one more time.

One temptation as you put your schedule together is to consider it as "carved in stone," and it can be very anxiety provoking to see that the project is getting off schedule. Instead, you have to view the schedule as a dynamic list such that when something changes, it may affect many subsequent dates that you have outlined. The important feature of the schedule is that it makes you aware of the implications of changes in the progress of your project and in the required adjustments in your activities.

Quality Controls

Although you may have a clear schedule and have much faith in those who are working for you, creating mechanisms to check the quality of the work being produced must be one of your primary concerns. There are lots of areas to be considered. Everything that is word processed must be sent through a spell checker program. All materials must be carefully proofread before they are sent to the printer. Ideally, proofreading will be done by both someone who is familiar with the project and also by someone who is not involved on a day to day basis. Also, be extremely careful about last-minute changes; sometimes in the rush to revise something the correction is made but a new error is created.

Much of the mail survey process involves stuffing envelopes with various materials and putting mailing labels on the envelopes. Sometimes the study involves relatively simple steps—insert a letter and a numbered questionnaire, put a mailing label on the envelope, seal it, put postage on the envelope, and mail it. However, even in these simple processes, things can go wrong. Someone can forget to insert a letter, someone can misnumber or forget to number a questionnaire, someone can mix up the labels such that the wrong label goes with the wrong questionnaire, the label can be put on crooked, the postage can be wrong or not put on at all, and the envelopes can be sent out without being sealed at all or with the seal not glued down well. You have to assume that if something can go wrong, it will go wrong sometimes. All of the above have happened at one point or another on projects I have worked on even though we were trying to be diligent.

The issues of potential mistakes can grow exponentially when the mailing process is more complicated or when the size of the study increases. As you get more steps to worry about or more people working on the mailing process, you have more opportunities for things to go wrong. One consideration that can help ensure the ultimate quality of your product is to analyze the work flow of the assembly process. Recently I was involved in a complex mailing for a study of employees at seven different companies. The envelopes had two letters (one from us and one from the respondent's company), a color-coded questionnaire that matched each company, about 10 different versions of each company questionnaire corresponding to different worksites within the seven companies, a return envelope, and a postage-paid return postcard with the respondents' names on it (which of course needed to match the label on the envelope).

As we analyzed the quality control issues and the efficiency considerations, we debated between a long assembly-line process (with each person doing one step) or a batch process in which each person took a worksite and did everything for it, or some other combinations. We chose the following mechanisms. First, we dealt with one company at a time; this meant that only one color questionnaire was going to be out on the table at a time. Second, we divided the assembly process into two stages.

The first stage involved inserting into the envelopes all the things that were common to that company using an assembly-line approach—the project letter, the company letter, the return envelope, and the right version of the questionnaire. Separate piles for each worksite, clearly marked, were made of each of these partially stuffed envelopes. The person who was supervising this process also served as quality checker. She made sure the appropriate number of worksite questionnaires were laid out for the assembly-line process, she reviewed a random sample of packets to make sure the contents were accurate, and she counted the finished packets to make sure there were the correct number.

In the second stage we completed the assembly process with the unique materials for that respondent—the postcard with his or her name on it and the corresponding label for the outgoing envelope. For this phase we had people working in three-person teams that dealt with one worksite at a time. One person would put the label on the envelope and one would put the matching label on the postcard. They would hand these two pieces to a third person sitting across the table from them who would check that they matched, insert the postcard, and seal the envelope. If we had enough work crew members on some days, we even had two teams working at once. This process seemed to work very efficiently and was extremely accurate. Our supervisor made sure each group had the proper batch of labels and counted to make sure there were the right number of completed packets.

The important message to take away from this example is to realize you should consciously analyze the steps involved in your assembly, think about the possible mistakes that could be made, and then design your processes in a way that minimizes the potential for mistakes as well as maximizing the potential for checking the work of others.

AESTHETICS

There are a variety of aesthetic issues that are important to attend to in the production of a mail survey (Blumenfeld, 1973; Ford, 1968). The reasons for worrying about these issues besides the inherent quest for beauty are that you will improve your response rates and the quality of your data. Response rates will be better because an aesthetically pleasing questionnaire is more likely to be considered important and competently prepared. Neat and stylish response alternatives and instructional messages make it easier for respondents to comply in a correct fashion.

Typesetting

In the days before word processors and desktop publishing programs, my recommendation for the final production of your questionnaire would be to have it typeset. The "clean," balanced, professional look of a typeset document was a very desirable image. Typesetting is still an option, but now word processing programs and particularly desktop publishing programs have the capability of producing the same quality product as typesetting would. The key is the skill of the person who is operating the programs and his or her sensitivity to and talent with aesthetic issues.

Balance

Each page of your questionnaire should be balanced. What I mean by that is that your margins at right and left and at top and bottom should be equal. Sometimes the way the sequence of questions runs, you wind up finishing a page three quarters of the way down, and the next question will not fit in the remaining space. It is important to make the page look complete by increasing the spacing between items on the page so that it looks balanced. The same goal is important if you have a two-column format. You want to make sure that both columns are equally "filled." In achieving balance it is better to have more white space around questions than it is to produce an overly crammed or squeezed look.

Type Style and Size

You should choose a typestyle that is "clean" looking rather than overly fancy or scripted. The key issue, however, is type size. Always use a type size that is large enough to be read easily. If your study is focusing on elderly respondents, then you may even want to incorporate a type size that is larger than normal. You also want to make judicious use of type style features such as boldfacing, underlining, or italicizing. In a sequence of questions that are very similar except one phrase, you may find it helpful to boldface that changing phrase. This helps the respondent pick up the difference in the questions on the first reading. You should not go overboard with this mechanism, however. If you use it in every question, then the respondents will tend to be unresponsive to its message.

Format of Questions

Every question should have a question number, either applied sequentially throughout the whole questionnaire or numbered sequentially within sections (e.g., A1, A2 .. B1, B2). By numbering each question you provide a mechanism that helps the respondent move through the questionnaire efficiently. Sometimes people are tempted with follow-up, probing questions to leave them unnumbered. I have found this to be a short-sighted strategy, because many respondents will accidentally skip unnumbered questions.

You also want to adopt a common style or format that you follow throughout the questionnaire. This style should encompass features such as the width of the margins, the number of spaces that you leave after the question number, and the number of lines between response categories. We have also used formats in which the questions themselves were done completely in boldfaced type and the response categories were done in regular type. This style also facilitates the respondents' eyescan from one question to the other.

Format of Response Categories

Response categories should also have an established style. You either want to display the categories vertically in one column or horizontally in one row. You should avoid if possible doubling up the categories into two columns or two rows. By using two columns or rows, you create an ambiguous sequence for the reading of the categories. In addition, if you have a sequence of questions that all use the same response categories, they should all be lined up vertically on the page. Again, these seemingly small formatting issues can make or break the image of your questionnaire.

The Physical Dimensions of the Questionnaire

Some have recommended that the questionnaire be produced on sheets of paper that are smaller than 8½ by 11 inches to give the appearance of a "small" task. In general, I am supportive of that notion *if* it does not conflict with some other formatting goals. For instance, the type size should not be made too small to compensate for the smaller page. Also, if the smaller pages result in significantly more pages, then it is not clear to me that there is a net benefit. Finally, smaller sized questionnaires then raise the issue of the size of the envelope. Standard sized envelopes are made for dealing with 8½-by-11-inch paper.

I definitely recommend the use of back-to-back printing of the pages because the weight of the paper is sufficient to keep the "backside" printing from bleeding through to the front of the page. Printing pages back to back cuts the number of sheets of paper in half, resulting in a questionnaire that looks "less weighty," which may help response rates. Postage costs also are reduced.

You want your questionnaire to look like a booklet, so you should have the printer run the pages off on 17-by-11-inch paper (two facing pages) and then fold them in the middle. The staples go right in the fold in a process called "saddle stitching."

Another style feature that has a direct influence on the number of pages in your questionnaire is using a two-column newspaper format. Many questions that have relatively short response categories (e.g., "yes/no" or "agree/disagree") can easily be placed in a two-column format. The question itself may take up a few extra lines because it cannot stretch all the way across the page, but the response categories take up no more space. Using this technique can reduce the number of pages in your questionnaire by anywhere from 25% to 50%.

Under no circumstances should a multiple-page, saddle-stitched, booklet questionnaire be folded in half or thirds to fit into a smaller envelope. Use the 9-by-12-inch envelopes for mailing so that the questionnaire can lie flat.

Return Envelopes

All mail surveys should include a postage-paid return envelope. This envelope should have your return address preprinted on it. The respondent should not have to fold the questionnaire in order for it to fit into the envelope. It may be necessary, however, for you to fold the return envelope in order for it to fit in the outgoing envelope.

A Professional Look

All of the "tips" on aesthetics are in pursuit of producing a questionnaire that has a "professional look" while also being easy to administer. If you spend the effort you will be rewarded with a better study. I have included some examples of different formats for questionnaires immediately following this page (Figures 8.1 and 8.2). See how each of them achieves a clean look, even though the specific decisions for formatting were different in each case.

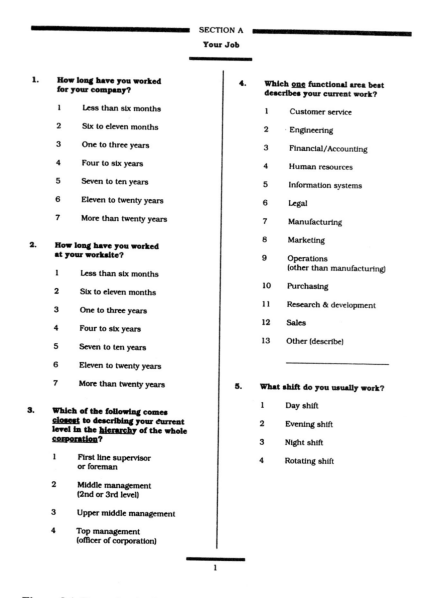

SECTION A

Your Job

1. **How long have you worked for your company?**

   1   Less than six months

   2   Six to eleven months

   3   One to three years

   4   Four to six years

   5   Seven to ten years

   6   Eleven to twenty years

   7   More than twenty years

2. **How long have you worked at your worksite?**

   1   Less than six months

   2   Six to eleven months

   3   One to three years

   4   Four to six years

   5   Seven to ten years

   6   Eleven to twenty years

   7   More than twenty years

3. **Which of the following comes closest to describing your current level in the hierarchy of the whole corporation?**

   1   First line supervisor or foreman

   2   Middle management (2nd or 3rd level)

   3   Upper middle management

   4   Top management (officer of corporation)

4. **Which one functional area best describes your current work?**

   1   Customer service

   2   Engineering

   3   Financial/Accounting

   4   Human resources

   5   Information systems

   6   Legal

   7   Manufacturing

   8   Marketing

   9   Operations (other than manufacturing)

   10   Purchasing

   11   Research & development

   12   Sales

   13   Other (describe)

   _____

5. **What shift do you usually work?**

   1   Day shift

   2   Evening shift

   3   Night shift

   4   Rotating shift

1

Figure 8.1. Example of a Questionnaire Format Giving a "Clean Look"

FUTURE DIRECTIONS IN AIDS EDUCATION

22. How much responsibility do you think each of the following groups should have in providing AIDS education?

	None	Minor	Moderate	Major
a. Parents	1□	2□	3□	4□
b. Teachers	1□	2□	3□	4□
c. Religious Organizations	1□	2□	3□	4□
d. Health Professionals	1□	2□	3□	4□

23. *Within the medical community*, what degree of responsibility should the following groups have in providing AIDS education?

	None	Minor	Moderate	Major
a. Physicians	1□	2□	3□	4□
b. Physician Assistants	1□	2□	3□	4□
c. Nurses	1□	2□	3□	4□
d. Health Educators/Family Planners	1□	2□	3□	4□
e. Social Workers	1□	2□	3□	4□

24. Should sterilized needles be provided to intravenous drug users?

   1□ Yes   2□ No

25. At what age should people first be educated about risk factors for AIDS? (check one)

   1□ under 9 years
   2□ 9 - 12 years
   3□ 13 - 15 years
   4□ 16 - 19 years
   5□ 20 years and older

26. Should condoms be made available at schools?

   1□ Yes   2□ No
        ↓

27. If *Yes*, what is the youngest grade level they should be made available?

   1□ Grade School (under 6th grade)
   2□ Junior High School (6th - 8th grade)
   3□ Senior High School (9th - 12th grade)
   4□ College (above 12th grade)

If there is anything else about AIDS education that you think is important, please use the space provided on the back. We appreciate the time and effort you have taken to answer our questions.

Please mail your questionnaire in the enclosed postage-paid envelope. Your postcard should be mailed separately. This will tell us that you have returned your questionnaire. Responses should be mailed by **April 1, 1988**. The return address is:

Dr. Thomas Mangione
Center for Survey Research
100 Arlington St.
Boston, MA 02116

THANK YOU FOR YOUR PARTICIPATION

Figure 8.2. Another Example of a Questionnaire Format With a "Clean Look"

9

Preparing the
Data for Analysis

In this chapter we will focus on processes that happen between the return of your questionnaires in the mail and the computer analyses that you will do to meet the study's objectives. We will discuss issues concerning coding and data entry as well as the rationale for building indices and scales out of your questions.

CODING CONVENTIONS

Coding refers to the process of assigning numerical equivalents to each answer for each question in your study. Actually, much of this process needs to be determined when you are developing your questionnaire. Some of the issues that we will raise go hand in hand with question development techniques. They also relate to format and presentation of your questions in the survey. Finally, many of the decisions you will make should be represented in your questionnaire before it goes to the printer.

Translating your data from the questionnaires to numerical values that the statistical programs on your computer need will be easier if "numerical codes" are attached to each answer category before the questionnaire is printed. In assigning these code values to the answer categories, you want to use the following conventions to maximize the efficiency and accuracy of the data entry process.

1. You want to number the answers such that the code values go in monotonically ascending or descending order. This will be easier to accomplish if your question categories are laid out in either a single vertical column or a single horizontal row. There are alternate approaches to numbering the categories illustrated below, and these raise two interesting considerations. You could number from 4 to 1, so the numbers would better reflect the meaning of the

categories: The big number corresponds to the greatest amount of satisfaction. A second alternative, 3 to 0, also creates a correspondence between the numbering system and the meaning of the categories. Not only is "3" the biggest number corresponding to the largest amount of satisfaction, but "0" reflects the meaning of "not at all satisfied." On the other hand, numbering the categories from "1" to "4" represents a natural progression and is perhaps a little easier for the data entry process.

1. VERY SATISFIED
2. SATISFIED
3. A LITTLE SATISFIED
4. NOT AT ALL SATISFIED

2. If you have more than nine response alternatives or if you think you may add some categories later, then you want to use a two-digit code (e.g., 01, 02, 03 . . . . 10, 11, 12).
3. You want to reserve a code value for a "don't know" answer even if there is no specific check box for that response. There will always be some respondents who will write in this type of answer. It is best to use a value that is likely to be used for this response in all of your questions. I tend to use an "8" value for a "don't know" or a "98" for a two-digit code or a "998" for a three-digit code.
4. You want to designate a code for an answer that should have been supplied but was "missing," "uninterpretable," or "not ascertained." I like to use a "9" or "99" or "." Obviously you will not have this type of code preprinted in your questionnaire, but instead it would be written in when you discover missing information.
5. You also need to designate a code for a question that you instructed the respondent to skip over. For instance, you might instruct respondents who say they do not have any children to skip over the section of questions asking about their children's education. Sometimes researchers even include a category for respondents to check across a series of questions that means "this question does not apply to me." Often this code will be written in after the questionnaires are returned. I like to use a "0" for this type of response.

The example in Figure 9.1 shows several different types of questions and the numerical values assigned to the answer categories.

━━━━━━━━━━━━━━━━ SECTION H ━━━━━━━━━━━━━━━━

Individual Background Characteristics

6. **In your work or home life, have you personally ever been involved in trying to get someone into treatment for an alcohol problem?**

    1   Yes, home and work
    2   Yes, home only
    3   Yes, work only
    4   No, neither

7. **Has there _ever_ been a time in your life when you thought that you had a drinking problem?**

    1   Yes
    2   No

8. **Have you ever referred an employee to your company-sponsored counseling or employee assistance program?**

    1   Yes
    2   No

9. **What is your current age?**

    1   Less than 30 years
    2   30 to 39 years
    3   40 to 49 years
    4   50 to 59 years
    5   60 or over

10. **What is your gender?**

    1   Male
    2   Female

11. **What is the highest level of education you completed?**

    1   Less than high school diploma
    2   High school diploma
    3   Some college or technical schooling beyond high school
    4   Four year college degree
    5   Graduate training/degree (masters or doctorate)

12. **What is your current marital status?**

    1   Never married
    2   Married
    3   Separated
    4   Widowed
    5   Divorced

13. **Approximately what is your annual gross salary from _your current job_?**

    1   Less than $20,000
    2    $20,000 to $39,999
    3    $40,000 to $59,999
    4    $60,000 to $79,999
    5    $80,000 to $99,999
    6    $100,000 to $149,999
    7    $150,000 or more

━━━━━━
13

Figure 9.1. Examples of Numerical Coding of Answers

DATA ENTRY

Methods of Transferring Data

There are several ways in which your data can actually get into the computer. The old-fashioned way was that you hired a team of "coders" to look at the answers to the surveys and transfer the code number of the answer to a sheet of paper that had 80 columns of boxes in a row. These 80 boxes corresponded to the 80 fields in a keypunch card. These sheets would then be sent to keypunching services, and the information would come back as a series of holes punched into these cards. You would then take these cards and "read" the data into the computer.

One great advance in this transfer process was made when the values for the answer categories were preprinted on the questionnaire, and little marginal notations were also printed that indicated column specifications (e.g., punch the answer to this question in column 37 of the card). This mechanism eliminated the step of people having to write each number onto a sheet before it was keypunched. You still needed to have people look over the questionnaires before they were sent to the keypunchers to "clean" them up and to add the 8s and 9s and 0s where needed. We call these people "editors."

Another advance was to use a direct data entry system to put the information directly into your computer. The advantage of this process is that you have direct control and supervision of the staff that is inputting the information. This gives you an opportunity to stay on top of the problems that arise during the entry process. In addition, there are several software programs that help you to individually tailor your entry routines such that effort is saved and many types of data entry mistakes are prevented. For instance, you can specify under what circumstances you automatically want a "0" punched in a series of columns (e.g., when unmarried respondents skip over the series of questions about marriage). You can also specify in these programs what the possible answers are; the program will not allow any other values to be punched in the corresponding column. This prevents any out-of-range values from appearing. Finally, these programs usually allow for blind, independent verification so that the quality of the keypunching can be ensured. The only drawbacks to these programs are that you have to buy them and you have to pay a staff to enter the information.

Any student who has taken a standardized exam like the SAT is familiar with another mechanism for transferring the information from the questionnaire to the computer—mark sensing scoring. This is a relatively inexpensive way to transfer the information if you have many questionnaires. For small amounts of questionnaires, the fixed costs of the scoring programming make this procedure more expensive than other alternatives. The only other issue that you have to consider is that you need to leave several weeks after your questionnaire is completed for the formatting and proofing of the machine readable forms. Before using this mechanism, you should also weigh the sample's tolerance of filling in bunches of little dots with a number 2 pencil. Samples of students and other groups like this are used to filling out such forms; other groups may find the procedure strange and alienating.

The Editing and Coding Process

All the data transferring mechanisms require at least some review or editing process before data are sent off to be converted into computer-usable form. Some respondents may not have answered questions that they were supposed to, others may have written in marginal comments instead of checking off a box, and others may have checked off multiple categories when the instructions were to select only one answer. These issues need to be resolved before questionnaires are sent off to the data entry process. Also, for whatever open-ended information may be in your questionnaire, the answers need to be converted into numerical codes before the data entry phase begins.

Whenever you have someone editing or coding your information in preparation for data entry, it is important to create a quality control system that reduces errors in decision making. The first step in designing your quality control system is to have a clear set of written instructions and coding rules before your editing/coding process begins. In addition, however, you want to confirm that your "editors/coders" are making reliable and valid decisions based on your instructions. To accomplish this you need to have a second person independently review or code a sample of each coder's work and compare the decisions made. Whenever there is a difference in the decision making, the difference needs to be resolved. Sometimes, these differences might point to an inadequacy in your decision rules. You would need to revise the rules before you get very far into your editing/coding task. In other instances, however, these disagreements would identify an editor/coder who did not understand your instructions or who was being sloppy with the work. Retraining and more detailed supervision of such coders' work is called for until you are convinced that they have the right idea.

Verification

Besides checking the editing/coding, you want to ensure that your data entry is being done correctly. The most common mechanism to ensure quality data entry is to request that the entry be "verified." In this process, a second person independently enters the information, and a comparison is made between what the first person entered and what the second person did. This mechanism is the only way to catch typos, for example a "1" accidentally being punched instead of a "2" when both answers are legitimate responses to the question. Differences between the two data enterers are resolved and corrected. This process should assure you that there are no errors in your data resulting from keystroke errors.

Cleaning Your Data

Usually two additional checks are made on your data before analyses begin. The first is to check for out-of-range responses; if your question answers are coded as "1," "2," or "3," you check to see that the only answers in your data are 1s, 2s, or 3s. If you have a stray "4" or "5" answer, then you need to pull out that questionnaire and check what the real answer should have been and make that change in your data.

The second check is a "consistency" check. Sometimes the answers to a particular question are determined by the answers to prior questions. For instance, early in the questionnaire you may ask if a person is married or not. Later, you may have an instruction that says: "answer this section if you are married, otherwise skip to the next section." For the people that skipped, the unmarried, you would code a "0" in this section of questions. You can check to make sure your data are consistent by making sure that everyone who was coded unmarried was given a "0" in the "marriage section of questions" and all marrieds were coded with the other possible code responses. If there are some inconsistencies, then you would pull these particular questionnaires and figure out how the data should have been coded.

Data entry software used by professional data entry services and also available to the individual researcher facilitate some of these error detection and prevention processes. For instance, these programs allow you to restrict certain values from being entered for specific questions. If the question answers are "1," "2," and "3" plus a "0" for skipped groups and an "8" for don't know and "9" for not ascertained, you can program the data entry software to not allow "4," "5," "6," or "7" to be entered in your data at this point. This out-of-range protection reduces many keystroke errors but of course cannot prevent a keystroke error that substitutes one legitimate value for another. Verification processes are still necessary.

The data entry software also helps with consistency errors. The software can be programmed to automatically insert "0s" for individuals who are not supposed to answer specific sequences of questions. The programs use conditional statements such as "if the respondent checked off a '1' response in question #10, then insert '0' for questions #11 through #20." Although this type of programming can prevent most types of inconsistency errors, it would still be useful to check these situations on your computer before going very far with your data analyses.

CREATING SCALES

Imagine that you have a series of questions in your questionnaire asking about satisfaction levels with various aspects of the respondent's job. It is a common procedure to combine the answers to these various questions into an overall score. It turns out that this process of aggregating information has several positive elements to it. First, you reduce the number of variables that you have to run analyses on; second, if done correctly such aggregation actually improves the reliability and potential validity of the measures in your study.

In general there are two ways to combine questions. You can either add the answers or you can take an average score. For either of these methods it is important that the scores of the answers have a similar range of values. Most people tend to treat each question that contributes to the overall score as equal unless there is some very specific rationale for counting one item more than other items. Most computer software analysis programs make it relatively easy to create these types of overall scores.

The only complication that you have to deal with is the fact that not every respondent will answer every question that you wish to combine. This means that some respondents have more chances to score "high" than other respondents. There are several strategies for dealing with this problem. If there are only a few cases missing some answers, you could decide to drop those cases from the analysis. If this is not feasible, then you could choose to construct an average score for each person based on the set of items answered. The specific set of items might vary slightly from respondent to respondent, but if you have a sound statistical basis for combining the items in the first place this turns out to be a reasonable strategy. Finally, you can do various estimation procedures, such as inserting the average of the other items that were answered for the missing information.

We mentioned above that by building indices you improve the reliability of your measures. Why is this so? The answer lies in the notion that each item in a questionnaire is a somewhat imperfect measure of the real construct we are actually interested in measuring. A large part of this imperfection may simply be random error (e.g., people accidentally checking the wrong box or a person feeling especially good or bad the day they filled out the questionnaire). By combining several imperfect measures, the random errors tend to cancel each other out, and the resulting "average" is a better estimate of the true state of affairs for that person.

There is a mathematical formula that will tell us how reliable our new combined measure is. It is called "coefficient alpha":

$$\alpha = \frac{(\text{number of items}) \times (\text{average correlation among items})}{1 + (\text{number of items} - 1) \times (\text{average correlation})}$$

Alpha increases with the number of items you combine (assuming no decrease in the average intercorrelation among the items) or if the average correlation is higher. For small numbers of items, alpha will still increase by adding items even if the average correlation goes down slightly because the improvement caused by increasing the number of items is greater than the decrement caused by a slight decrease in the average correlation among the items.

10

A Summary From a Total Survey Design Perspective

TOTAL SURVEY DESIGN

Now that you have reached the end of this book, it is important to put all the facets together and to have them all work for you to produce a high quality survey. In each chapter that precedes this one, we have focused on one part of the survey process and tried to give you an in-depth understanding of the issues and procedures to follow. In the real world, one rarely gets the opportunity to conduct an "ideal" project—one where quality is maximized at each decision point. Instead each project is a series of trade-offs and balancing efforts that tries to produce an optimum combination of decisions that produces the best total quality.

This process of trying to achieve an optimum balance is called a "total survey design" approach. An example of an inadequate attempt to apply the principles of total survey design would be a project in which a multistage, random sample of households was developed (very expensive but accurate) and used for a mail survey in which there were no follow-up reminders sent (cheap but probably biased). What this example emphasizes is that it does not do your project any good to put all or most of your resources into one phase and in so doing leave inadequate resources to undertake the other phases.

In this chapter we want to accomplish two things. First, we want to review the decisions that you will be making in producing a mail survey to emphasize the issues that need to be brought into balance. Second, we want to lay out a sequence of steps that you would need to follow in each of the major phases of the project. By following both sets of guidelines you could design your own study in a way that optimizes the quality of your efforts.

Sampling Frame

Your sample is only as good as your sampling frame (the list from which you select your sample). Leaving part of the population out creates bias. How large the bias is often is unknown. The decisions that you have to make at this phase are (a) what is the population that you want to study, (b) what are the alternate ways in which a list of that population can be obtained, and (c) how adequately does each of these ways reflect the total membership in that population?

Sometimes you can easily get access to a good list, but the list very specifically leaves out a group of people in the population. Some examples of good lists that leave people out are phone books that leave out people without phones and people who have unlisted numbers, the registry of motor vehicles leaving out people who do not have driver's licenses, and the registrar's office only having a list of currently enrolled students. In each of these examples, you have to decide whether the groups that are left out are important to your study. If they are, then you have to look for another list; if they are not, then the list may be acceptable for your needs. At least you should be clear what types of people you are leaving out of your study so that you can be accurate with your written description of your sample.

Sample Size

Remember that quadrupling your sample size will cut your sampling error in half. Also remember that the biggest gains in the reduction of sampling error occur when the sample size is small and the proportion change in sample size that you contemplate is relatively large. Before you can make any decisions about sample size, you have to know what your major analytic questions are. This is the only way to be sure that the size of your sample will support your analysis plans. You have to decide how precise you want your estimates to be and make sample size determinations accordingly.

Sample Design

There are several design decisions that you have to make. First, should your sample be a random sample, or should you use a convenience or quota sample design? There are some exploratory purposes that could be served well enough by using nonrandom sampling designs. You need to figure out what goals you are trying to accomplish in conducting this study.

Second, you need to decide whether you can set up any stratification in your sample list, and if you can, on which variables you want to stratify. Stratification of your list is always good because it helps reduce sampling error. To be able to use stratification, the necessary information for sorting your list has to be attached to the original list.

Stratification also enables you to oversample small but important subgroups. There is some cost to this in that your effective overall sample size for statistical considerations is reduced somewhat after you weight to compensate for the higher sampling rates.

Measurement Error

Sampling error is not the only source of error in your study. It is critical that you spend time, energy, and resources to ensure that your questions are written and presented so as to minimize measurement error. Primarily this means striving to create questions that are clear and that ask the respondent to do tasks that are reasonable. Pretesting, revising, and pretesting again are essential components in this process. Almost every study could benefit from more pretesting.

Besides clarity, pretesting can help you resolve issues such as:

1. how many response categories you should have,
2. whether the response categories represent reasonably spaced increments,
3. whether you should use an odd or even number of categories,
4. whether you want to use a "don't know" category,
5. is the recall period a reasonable length,
6. is the question too intrusive,
7. whether the vast majority of people can answer the question, and
8. if there is a reasonable distribution of answers across the response alternatives.

Designing a pretest process that allows you to talk with pretest respondents and to directly assess their understanding of the question is essential to gaining appropriate feedback.

Nonresponse Error

The biggest potential problem with conducting mail surveys is nonresponse error. The people who respond to your survey may be different from the people who chose not to respond. The most effective way to deal with nonresponse error is to obtain as high a response rate as feasible. You need to figure out what kinds of strategies you are going to use to make your response rate as high as is feasible. The most certain way to improve your response rate is to create a good respondent letter, include a postage-paid envelope, and send out reminders. Beyond these, you should use as many of the following as feasible.

1. Use some type of prepaid incentive.
2. Keep the length of your survey reasonable.
3. Design the survey so that it looks neat and aesthetically pleasing.
4. Use pretty commemorative stamps on the return envelopes.
5. Prenotify your respondents that they have been selected to be in a survey, preferably by telephone.
6. Use some type of premium postage mechanism to deliver at least the last reminder.
7. Use colored paper for the cover of your questionnaire.

Coding and Data Entry

As the questionnaires are transformed from written responses to computer numbers, the concerns for standardization and quality control that we emphasized in other phases must again be realized. You need to create codes that are easy to apply. You also need to train your editors well and to supervise their use of your coding rules by reviewing a significant proportion of their work early in the process. Data entry should always be 100% verified. On top of these processes, when your computer file is being constructed you need to run tests to discover out-of-range punches and inconsistent data elements. These errors need to be checked against the original questionnaires and then corrected.

Total Survey Design Summary

Again we want to emphasize that a quality mail survey effort requires that you optimize your efforts in all phases of the research project. You need to devote resources to each of the decision areas summarized above. Errors can appear in your data at each phase. You have to make decisions that will help you minimize errors at each juncture. One of the most common mistakes in survey research work is to act as if the only source of errors is sampling error and to put so much of the resources into creating a large number of returns that resources are inadequate to attend to other issues.

TIME LINES

Planning and allocation of resources are necessary components in creating a survey effort that goes as smoothly as is possible. This is not to say that once the plan is made you carve it in stone. Things do change. Some things take longer to do than others, and sometimes there are unexpected foul-ups with delivery of materials. If you have a clear plan with a well-thought-out time line, at least you can assess the impact of these unexpected problems. To that end we offer the following time lines to help you with your planning process (see Figures 10.1 to 10.6). The first time lines show you how the overall project fits together. The detailed time lines that follow focus on each of the major phases and call attention to key points.

CLOSING THOUGHTS

Although I expect this book to help you in producing high quality mail surveys, I am also the first to acknowledge that experience is a wonderful teacher. I would highly recommend that when venturing out for your first few surveys, you build access to someone who has had a lot of experience with surveys and use that person to help you plan, review, edit, and revise. Do not be afraid to have someone tell you that something can be improved; no one ever gets to the point where efforts are immune to a good suggestion.

The indefatigable pursuit of an unattainable perfection even though it consist in nothing more than in the pounding of an old piano, is what alone gives a meaning to our lives on this unavailing star.

Logan-Pearsall Smith
1865-1946
Anglo American Essayist

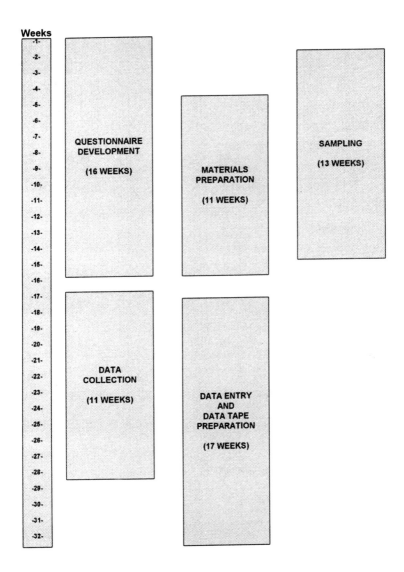

Figure 10.1. Overall Time Line

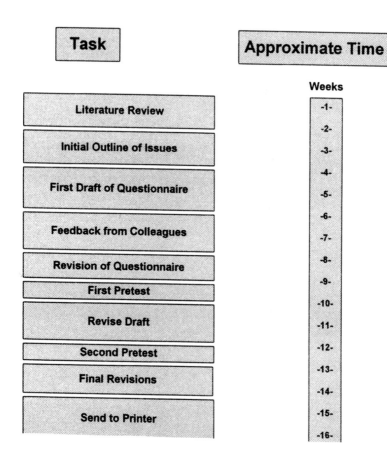

Figure 10.2. Time Line for Questionnaire Development

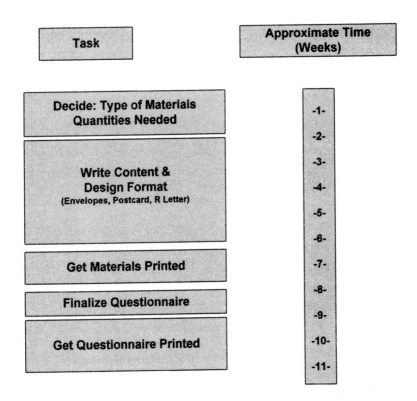

Figure 10.3. Time Line for Sampling

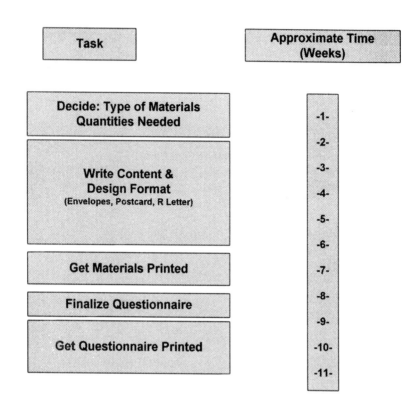

Figure 10.4. Time Line for Materials Preparation

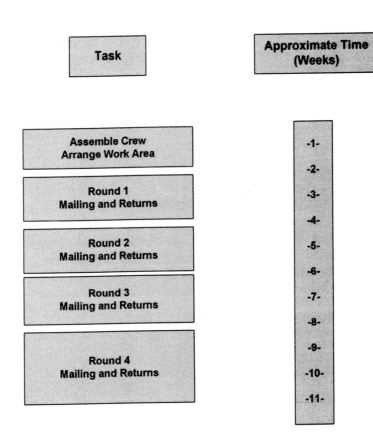

Figure 10.5. Time Line for Data Collection

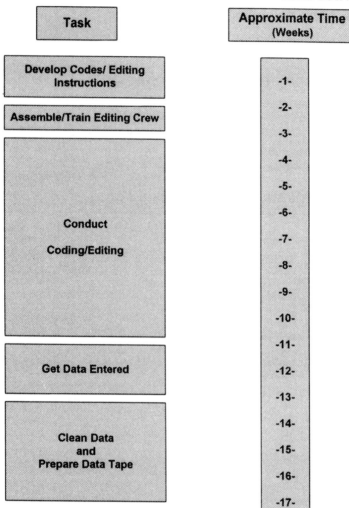

Figure 10.6. Time Line for Coding/Data Entry

References

Adams, J. S. (1956). Experiment on question and response bias. *Public Opinion Quarterly, 20,* 593-598.

Adams, L. L. M., & Gale, D. (1982). Solving the quandary between questionnaire length and response rate in educational research. *Research in Higher Education, 17,* 231-240.

Allen, C. T., Schewe, C. D., & Wijk, G. (1980). More on self-perception theory's foot technique in the pre-call/mail survey setting. *Journal of Marketing Research, 17,* 498-502.

Andreasen, A. R. (1970). Personalizing mail questionnaire correspondence. *Public Opinion Quarterly, 34,* 273-277.

Armstrong, J. S. (1975). Monetary incentives in mail surveys. *Public Opinion Quarterly, 39,* 111-116.

Armstrong, J. S., & Lusk, E. J. (1987). Return postage in mail surveys. *Public Opinion Quarterly, 51,* 233-248.

Armstrong, J. S., & Overton, T. S. (1971). Brief versus comprehensive descriptions in measuring intentions to purchase. *Journal of Marketing Research, 8,* 114-117.

Armstrong, J. S., & Overton, T. S. (1977). Estimating nonresponse bias in mail surveys. *Journal of Marketing Research, 14,* 396-402.

Ayidiya, S. A., & McClendon, M. J. (1990). Response effects in mail surveys. *Public Opinion Quarterly, 54,* 229-247.

Bachman, D. P. (1987). Cover letter appeals and sponsorship effects on mail survey response rates. *Journal of Marketing Education, 92,* 45-51.

Barnette, W. L. (1950). Non-respondent problem in questionnaire research. *Journal of Applied Psychology, 34,* 397-398.

Baur, E. J. (1947). Response bias in a mail survey. *Public Opinion Quarterly, 11,* 594-600.

Berdie, D. R. (1973). Questionnaire length and response rate. *Journal of Applied Psychology, 58,* 278-280.

Berry, S., & Kanouse, D. (1987). Physicians' response to a mailed survey: An experiment in timing of payment. *Public Opinion Quarterly, 51,* 102-104.

Biemer, P. R., Groves, R. M., Lyberg, L. E., Mathiowetz, N. A., & Sudman, S. (1991). *Measurement errors in surveys.* New York: John Wiley.

Bishop, G. F., Hippler, H. J., Schwartz, N., & Strack, F. (1988). Comparison of response effects in self-administered and telephone surveys. In R. M. Groves, P. Biemer, L. Lyberg, J. Massey, W. Nicholls, & J. Waksberg (Eds.), *Telephone Survey Methodology* (pp. 321-340). New York: John Wiley.

Bishop, G. F., Oldendick, R. W., & Tuchfarber, A. J. (1984). Interest in political campaigns: The influence of question order and electoral context. *Political Behavior, 6,* 159-169.

Blair, W. S. (1964). How subject matter can bias a mail survey. *Mediascope,* 70-72.

Blumberg, H. H., Fuller, C., & Hare, A. P. (1974). Response rates in postal surveys. *Public Opinion Quarterly, 38,* 113-123.

Blumenfeld, W. S. (1973). Effect of appearance of corresponding on response rate to a mail questionnaire. *Psychological Reports, 32,* 178.

Boek, W. E., & Lade, J. H. (1963). Test of the usefulness of the postcard technique in a mail questionnaire study. *Public Opinion Quarterly, 27,* 303-306.

Bradt, K. (1955). Usefulness of a postcard technique in a mail questionnaire study. *Public Opinion Quarterly, 19,* 218-222.

Brennan, M., & Hoek, J. (1992). Behavior of respondents, nonrespondents and refusers across mail surveys. *Public Opinion Survey, 56,* 530-535.

Brennan, M., Hoek, J., & Astridge, C. (1991). Effects of monetary incentives on the response rate and cost-effectiveness of a mail survey. *Journal of the Market Research Society, 33,* 229-241.

Brennan, R. (1958). Trading stamps as an incentive. *Journal of Marketing, 22,* 306-307.

Brook, L. L. (1978). Effect of different postage combinations on response levels and speed of reply. *Journal of the Market Research Society, 20,* 238-244.

Brunner, A. G., & Carroll, S. J., Jr. (1969). Effect of prior notification on the refusal rate in fixed address Surveys. *Journal of Advertising Research, 9,* 42-44.

Bryson, M. C. (1976). Literacy Digest Poll: Making of a statistical myth. *American Statistician, 30,* 184-185.

Burchell, B., & Marsh, C. (1992). Effect of questionnaire length on survey response. *Quality and Quantity, 26,* 233-244.

Campbell, D. T. (1949). Bias in mail surveys. *Public Opinion Quarterly, 13,* 562.

Carpenter, E. H. (1975). Personalizing mail surveys: A replication and reassessment. *Public Opinion Quarterly, 38,* 614-620.

Champion, D. J., & Sear, A. M. (1969). Questionnaire response rates: A methodological analysis. *Social Forces, 47,* 335-339.

Childers, T. L., & Ferrell, O. C. (1979). Response rates and perceived questionnaire length in mail surveys. *Journal of Marketing Research, 16,* 429-431.

Childers, T. L., Pride, W. M., & Ferrell, O. C. (1980). Reassessment of the effects of appeals on response to mail surveys. *Journal of Marketing Research, 17,* 365-370.

Childers, T. L., & Skinner, S. J. (1985). Theoretical and empirical issues in the identification of survey respondents. *Journal of the Market Research Society, 27,* 39-53.

Clausen, J. A., & Ford, R. N. (1947). Controlling bias in mail questionnaires. *Journal of the American Statistical Association, 42,* 497-511.

Cohen, J. (1988). *Statistical power analysis for the behavioral sciences.* Hillsdale, NJ: Lawrence Erlbaum.

Converse, J. M., & Presser, S. (1986). *Survey questions: Handcrafting the standardized questionnaire.* Beverly Hills, CA: Sage.

Cox, E. P., III. (1976). Cost/benefit view of prepaid monetary incentives in mail questionnaires. *Public Opinion Quarterly, 40,* 101-104.

Cox, E. P., III, Anderson, Jr., W. T., & Fulcher, D. G. (1974). Reappraising mail survey response rates. *Journal of Marketing Research, 11,* 413-417.

Craig, C. S., & McCann, J. M. (1978). Item nonresponse in mail surveys: Extent and correlates. *Journal of Marketing Research, 15,* 285-289.

Church, A. H. (1993). Estimating the effect of incentives on mail survey response rates: A meta analysis. *Public Opinion Quarterly, 57,* 62-79.

Daniel, W. W. (1975). Nonresponse in sociological surveys: A review of some methods for handling the problem. *Sociological Methods & Research, 3,* 291-307.

Denton, J., Tsai, C., & Chevrette, P. (1988). Effects on survey responses of subject, incentives, and multiple mailings. *Journal of Experimental Education, 56,* 77-82.

Dillman, D., Carpenter, E., Christenson, J., & Brooks, R. (1974). Increasing mail questionnaire response: A four state comparison. *American Sociological Review, 39,* 744-756.

Dillman, D. A. (1972). Increasing mail questionnaire response in large samples of the general public. *Public Opinion Quarterly, 36,* 254-257.

Dillman, D. A. (1978). *Mail and telephone surveys: The total design method.* New York: John Wiley.

Dillman, D. A., & Frey, J. H. (1974). Contribution of personalization to mail questionnaire response as an element of a previously tested method. *Journal of Applied Psychology, 59,* 297-301.

Dommeyer, C. (1988). How form of the monetary incentive affects mail survey response. *Journal of the Market Research Society, 30,* 379-385.

Dommeyer, C. J. (1985). Does response to an offer of mail survey results interact with questionnaire interest? *Journal of the Market Research Society, 27,* 27-38.

Donald, M. N. (1960). Implications of non-response for the interpretation of mail questionnaire data. *Public Opinion Quarterly, 24,* 99-114.

Doob, A. N., Freedman, J. L., & Carlsmith, J. M. (1973). Effects of sponsor and prepayment on compliance with a mailed request. *Journal of Applied Psychology, 57,* 346-347.

Duncan, W. J. (1979). Mail questionnaires in survey research: A review of response inducement techniques. *Journal of Management, 5,* 39-55.

Eckland, B. (1965). Effects of prodding to increase mail back returns. *Journal of Applied Psychology, 49,* 165-169.

Eichner, K., & Habermehl, W. (1981). Predicting response rates to mailed questionnaires. *American Sociological Review, 46,* 361-363.

Etzel, M. J., & Walker, B. J. (1974). Effects of alternative follow-up procedures on mail survey response rates. *Journal of Applied Psychology, 59,* 219-221.

Ferris, A. L. (1951). Note on stimulating response to questionnaires. *American Sociological Review, 16,* 247-249.

Filion, F. L. (1975). Estimating bias due to nonresponse in mail surveys. *Public Opinion Quarterly, 39,* 482-492.

Filion, F. L. (1976). Exploring and correcting for nonresponse bias using follow-ups on nonrespondents. *Pacific Sociological Review, 19,* 401-408.

Ford, N. M. (1967). The advance letter in mail surveys. *Journal of Marketing Research, 4,* 202-204.

Ford, N. M. (1968). Questionnaire appearance and response rates in mail surveys. *Journal of Advertising Research, 8,* 43-45.

Ford, R. N., & Zeisel, H. (1949). Bias in mail surveys cannot be controlled by one mailing. *Public Opinion Quarterly, 13,* 495-501.

Fowler, F. J. (1993). *Survey research methods.* Newbury Park, CA: Sage.

Fowler, F. J. (1995). *Improving survey questions: Design and evaluation.* Thousand Oaks, CA: Sage.

Fox, R. J., Crask, M. R., & Kim, J. (1988). Mail survey response rate: A meta-analysis of selected techniques for inducing response. *Public Opinion Quarterly, 52,* 467-491

Frazier, G., & Bird, K. (1958). Increasing the response of a mail questionnaire. *Journal of Marketing, 22,* 186-187.

Friedman, H. M., & San Augustine, A. J. (1979). The effects of a monetary incentive and the ethnicity of the sponsor's signature on the rate and quality of response to a mail survey. *Journal of the Academy of Marketing Science, 7,* 95-101.

Fuller, C. (1974). Effect of anonymity on return rate and response bias in a mail survey. *Journal of Applied Psychology, 59,* 292-296.

Furse, D. H., & Stewart, D. W. (1982). Monetary incentives versus promised contribution to charity: New evidence on mail survey response. *Journal of Marketing Research, 19,* 375-380.

Furse, D. H., Stewart, D. W., & Rados, D. L. (1981). Effects of foot-in-the-door, cash incentives, and followups on survey response. *Journal of Marketing Research, 18,* 473-478.

Futrell, C., & Hise, R. T. (1982). The effects of anonymity and a same-day deadline on the response rate to mail surveys. *European Research, 10,* 171-175.

Futrell, C., & Swan, J. E. (1977). Anonymity and response by salespeople to a mail questionnaire. *Journal of Marketing Research, 14,* 611-616.

Gajraj, A. M., Faria, A. J., & Dickinson, J. R. (1990). Comparison of the effect of promised and provided lotteries, monetary and gift incentives on mail survey response rate, speed and cost. *Journal of the Market Research Society, 32,* 141-162.

Gannon, M., Northern, J., & Carrol, S., Jr. (1971). Characteristics of non-respondents among workers. *Journal of Applied Psychology, 55,* 586-588.

Gelb, B. D. (1975). Incentives to increase survey returns: Social class considerations. *Journal of Marketing Research, 12,* 107-109.

Godwin, K. (1979). Consequences of large monetary incentives in mail surveys of elites. *Public Opinion Quarterly, 43,* 378-387.

Goodstadt, M. S., Chung, L., Kronitz, R., & Cook, G. (1977). Mail survey response rates: Their manipulation and impact. *Journal of Marketing Research, 14,* 391-395.

Gough, H. G., & Hall, W. B. (1977). Comparison of physicians who did and did not respond to a postal questionnaire. *Journal of Applied Psychology, 62,* 777-780.

Gullahorn, J. E., & Gullahorn, J. T. (1963). An investigation of the effects of three factors on response to mail questionnaires. *Public Opinion Quarterly, 27,* 294-296.

Hackler, J. C., & Bourgette, P. (1973). Dollars, dissonance, and survey returns. *Public Opinion Quarterly, 37,* 276-281.

Hancock, J. W. (1940). An experimental study of four methods of measuring unit costs of obtaining attitude toward the retail store. *Journal of Applied Psychology, 24,* 213-230.

Hansen, R. A. (1980). A self-perception interpretation of the effect of monetary and non-monetary incentives on mail survey respondent behavior. *Journal of Marketing Research, 17,* 77-83.

Harris, J. R., & Guffey, H. J., Jr. (1978). Questionnaire returns: Stamps versus business reply envelopes revisited. *Journal of Marketing Research, 15,* 290-293.

Heaton, E. E., Jr. (1965). Increasing mail questionnaire returns with a preliminary letter. *Journal of Advertising Research, 5,* 36-39.

Heberlein, T. A., & Baumgartner, R. (1978). Factors affecting response rates to mailed questionnaires: A quantitative analysis of the published literature. *American Sociological Review, 43,* 447-462.

Hendrick, C. R., Borden, R., Giesen, M., Murray, E. J., & Seyfried, B. A. (1972). Effectiveness of ingratiation tactics in a cover letter on mail questionnaire response. *Psychonomic Science, 26,* 349-351.

Henley, J. R., Jr. (1976). Response rate to mail questionnaires with a return deadline. *Public Opinion Quarterly, 40,* 374-375.

Hite, S. (1976). *Hite report: A nationwide study of female sexuality.* New York: Macmillan.

Hopkins, K. D., & Gullickson, A. R. (1992). Response rates in survey research: A meta-analysis of the effects of monetary gratuities. *Journal of Experimental Education, 61,* 52-62.

Hopkins, K. D., & Podolak, J. (1983). Class-of-mail and the effects of monetary gratuity on the response rates of mailed questionnaires. *Journal of Experimental Education, 51*, 169-170.

Hornik, J. (1981). Time cue and time perception effect on response to mail surveys. *Journal of Marketing Research, 18*, 243-248.

House, J. S., Gerber, W., & McMichael, A. J. (1977). Increasing mail questionnaire response: A controlled replication and extension. *Public Opinion Quarterly, 41*, 95-99.

Houston, M. J., & Jefferson, R. W. (1975). The negative effects of personalization on response patterns in mail surveys. *Journal of Marketing Research, 12*, 114-117.

Houston, M. J., & Nevin, J. R. (1977). The effects of source and appeal on mail survey response patterns. *Journal of Marketing Research, 14*, 374-377.

Hubbard, R., & Little, E. (1988). Promised contributions to charity and mail survey responses replication with extension. *Public Opinion Quarterly, 52*, 223-230.

Huck, S. W., & Gleason, E. M. (1974). Using monetary inducements to increase response rate from mailed surveys. *Journal of Applied Psychology, 59*, 222-225.

James, J. M., & Bolstein, R. (1990). Effect of monetary incentives and follow-up mailings on the response rate and response quality in mail surveys. *Public Opinion Quarterly, 54*, 346-361.

James, J. M., & Bolstein, R. (1992). Large monetary incentives and their effect on mail survey response rates. *Public Opinion Quarterly, 56*, 442-453.

Jolson, M. A. (1977). How to double or triple mail response rates. *Journal of Marketing, 41*, 78-81.

Jones, W. H., & Lang, J. R. (1980). Sample composition bias and response bias in a mail survey: A comparison of inducement methods. *Journal of Marketing Research, 17*, 69-76.

Jones, W. H., & Linda, G. (1978). Multiple criteria effects in a mail survey experiment. *Journal of Marketing Research, 15*, 280-284.

Kanuk, L., & Berenson, C. (1975). Mail surveys and response rates: A literature review. *Journal of Marketing Research, 12*, 440-453.

Kawash, M. B., & Aleamoni, L. M. (1971). Effect of personal signature on the initial rate of return of a mailed questionnaire. *Journal of Applied Psychology, 55*, 589-592.

Kephart, W. M., & Bressler, M. (1958). Increasing the responses to mail questionnaires. *Public Opinion Quarterly, 22*, 123-132.

Kerin, R. A., & Peterson, R. A. (1977). Personalization, respondent anonymity, and response distortion in mail surveys. *Journal of Applied Psychology, 62*, 86-89.

Kernan, J. B. (1971). Are "Bulk Rate Occupants" really unresponsive? *Public Opinion Quarterly, 35*, 420-424.

Kimball, A. E. (1961). Increasing the rate of return in mail surveys. *Journal of Marketing, 25*, 63-65.

Larson, R. F., & Catton, W. R., Jr. (1959). Can the mail-back bias contribute to a study's validity? *American Sociological Review, 24*, 243-245.

Lavrakas, P. J. (1993). *Telephone survey methods: Sampling, selecton and supervision* (2nd ed.). Newbury Park, CA: Sage.

Linsky, A. S. (1975). Stimulating responses to mailed questionnaires: A review. *Public Opinion Quarterly, 39*, 82-101.

Lockhart, D. C. (1991). Mailed surveys to physicians: The effect of incentives and length on the return rate. *Journal of Pharmaceutical Marketing & Management, 6*, 107-121.

Lorenzi, P., Friedmann, R., & Paolillo, J. (1988). Consumer mail survey responses: More (unbiased) bang for the buck. *Journal of Consumer Marketing, 5,* 31-40.

Martin, J. D., & McConnell, J. P. (1970). Mail questionnaire response induction: The effect of four variables on the response of a random sample to a difficult questionnaire. *Social Science Quarterly, 51,* 409-414.

Mason, W. S., Dressel, R. J., & Bain, R. K. (1961). An experimental study of factors affecting response to a mail survey of beginning teachers. *Public Opinion Quarterly, 25,* 296-299.

McCrohan, K. F., & Lowe, L. S. (1981). A cost/benefit approach to postage used on mail questionnaires. *Journal of Marketing, 45,* 130-133.

McDaniel, S. W., & Jackson, R. W. (1981). An investigation of respondent anonymity's effect on mailed questionnaire response rate and quality. *Journal of the Market Research Society, 23,* 150-160.

Myers, J. H., & Haug, A. F. (1969). How a preliminary letter affects mail survey return and costs. *Journal of Advertising Research, 9,* 37-39.

Nederhof, A. J. (1983). The effects of material incentives in mail surveys: Two studies. *Public Opinion Quarterly, 47,* 103-111.

Nevin, J. R., & Ford, N. M. (1976). Effects of a deadline and a veiled threat on mail survey responses. *Journal of Applied Psychology, 61,* 116-118.

Newman, S. W. (1962). Differences between early and late respondents to a mailed survey. *Journal of Advertising Research, 2,* 37-39.

Ognibene, P. (1970). Traits affecting questionnaire response. *Journal of Advertising Research, 10,* 18-20.

O'Keefe, T., & Homer, P. (1987). Selecting cost-effective survey methods: Foot-in-the-door and prepaid monetary incentives. *Journal of Business Research, 15,* 365-376.

Parsons, R. J., & Medford, T. S. (1972). The effect of advanced notice in mail surveys of homogeneous groups. *Public Opinion Quarterly, 36,* 258-259.

Pearlin, L. I. (1961). The appeals of anonymity in questionnaire response. *Public Opinion Quarterly, 25,* 640-647.

Peterson, R. A. (1975). An experimental investigation of mail-survey responses. *Journal of Business Research, 3,* 199-209.

Pressley, M. M., & Tullar, W. L. (1977). A factor interactive investigation of mail survey response rates from a commercial population. *Journal of Marketing Research, 14,* 108-111.

Price, D. O. (1950). On the use of stamped return envelopes with mail questionnaires. *American Sociological Review, 15,* 672-673.

Pucel, D. J., Nelson, H. F., & Wheeler, D. N. (1971). Questionnaire follow-up returns as a function of incentives and responder characteristics. *Vocational Guidance Quarterly, 19,* 188-193.

Reuss, C. F. (1943). Differences between persons responding and not responding to a mailed questionnaire. *American Sociological Review, 8,* 433-438.

Roberts, R. E., McCrory, O. F., & Forthofer, R. N. (1978). Further evidence on using a deadline to stimulate responses to a mail survey. *Public Opinion Quarterly, 42,* 407-410.

Robertson, D. H., & Bellenger, D. N. (1978). A new method of increasing mail survey responses: Contributions to charity. *Journal of Marketing Research, 15,* 632-633.

Robins, L. N. (1963). The reluctant respondent. *Public Opinion Quarterly, 27,* 276-286.

Roeher, G. A. (1963). Effective techniques in increasing response to mail questionnaires. *Public Opinion Quarterly, 27,* 299-302.

Roscoe, A. M., Lang, D., & Sheth, J. N. (1975). Follow-up methods, questionnaire length, and market differences in mail surveys. *Journal of Marketing, 39,* 20-27.

Rosen, N. (1960). Anonymity and attitude measurement. *Public Opinion Quarterly, 24,* 675-680.

Rucker, M., Hughes, R., Thompson, R., Harrison, A., & Vanderlip, N. (1984). Personalization of mail surveys: Too much of a good thing? *Educational and Psychological Measurement, 44,* 893-905.

Schegelmilch, B. B., & Diamantopoulos, S. (1991). Prenotification and mail survey response rates: A quantitative integration of the literature. *Journal of the Market Research Society, 33,* 243-255.

Schewe, C. D., & Cournoyer, N. D. (1976). Prepaid vs. promised incentives to questionnaire response: Further evidence. *Public Opinion Quarterly, 40,* 105-107.

Schuman, H., Kalton, G., & Ludwig, J. (1983). Context and continuity in survey questionnaires. *Public Opinion Quarterly, 47,* 112-115.

Schuman, H., & Presser, S. (1981). *Questions and answers in attitude surveys: Experiments in question form, wording and context.* New York: Academic Press.

Schuman, H., & Scott, J. (1987). Problems in the use of survey questions to measure public opinion. *Science, 236,* 957-959.

Scott, C. (1961). Research on mail surveys. *Journal of the Royal Statistical Society, Series A, Part 2, 124,* 143-205.

Simon, R. (1967). Responses to personal and form letters in mail surveys. *Journal of Advertising Research, 7,* 28-30.

Sletto, R. F. (1940). Pretesting of questionnaires. *American Sociological Review, 5,* 193-200.

Stafford, J. E. (1966). Influence of preliminary contact on mail returns. *Journal of Marketing Research, 3,* 410-411.

Suchman, E. A. (1962). An analysis of "bias" in survey research. *Public Opinion Quarterly, 26,* 102-111.

Suchman, E. A., & McCandless, B. (1940). Who answers questionnaires? *Journal of Applied Psychology, 24,* 758-769.

Vocino, T. (1977). Three variables in stimulating responses to mailed questionnaires. *Journal of Marketing, 41,* 76-77.

Walker, B. J., & Burdick, R. K. (1977). Advance correspondence and error in mail surveys. *Journal of Marketing Research, 14,* 379-382.

Watson, J. (1965). Improving the response rate in mail research. *Journal of Advertising Research, 5,* 48-50.

Weilbacher, W., & Walsh, H. R. (1952). Mail questionnaires and the personalized letter of transmittal. *Journal of Marketing, 16,* 331-336.

Wildman, R. C. (1977). Effects of anonymity and social settings on survey responses. *Public Opinion Quarterly, 41,* 74-79.

Wotruba, T. R. (1966). Monetary inducements and mail questionnaire response. *Journal of Marketing Research, 3,* 398-400.

Wynn, G. W., & McDaniel, S. W. (1985). The effect of alternative foot-in-the-door manipulations on mailed questionnaire response rate and quality. *Journal of the Market Research Society, 27,* 15-26.

Yammarino, F. J., Skinner, S. J., & Childers, T. L. (1991). Understanding mail survey response behavior. *Public Opinion Quarterly, 55,* 613-639.

Yu, J., & Cooper, H. (1983). A quantitative review of research design effects on response rates to questionnaires. *Journal of Marketing Research, 20,* 36-44.

INDEX

About the Author

Thomas W. Mangione is a senior research scientist at JSI Research and Training Institute in Boston. He obtained his Ph.D. in organizational psychology from the University of Michigan in 1973. As a graduate student he worked on several national surveys of employment at Michigan's Survey Research Center. He has had more than 25 years of survey research experience using in-person, telephone, and self-administered data collection modes. Before joining JSI he worked as a senior research fellow at the University of Massachusetts' Center for Survey Research. There he worked on more than 100 different survey projects spanning a wide range of topics including environmental health risks, alcohol use, AIDS knowledge and risk behaviors, crime and fear, and mental health. He had many occasions to consult with other researchers on their questionnaire and study design issues. While at JSI, he continued his work concerning alcohol use, AIDS needs assessments, and a variety of consultations on questionnaire design. Dr. Mangione has published several articles and another book in this series on survey research methodology (*Standardized Survey Interviewing* with Floyd J. Fowler, Jr.). He also teaches classes in survey research methodology at both the Boston University and Harvard University Schools of Public Health.